Day Trading Made Easy 2022

Beginner's Guide to Making Money Every Day with Day Trading

© Copyright 2022- All rights reserved.

The content contained within this book may not be reproduced, duplicated or transmitted without direct written permission from the author or the publisher. Under no circumstances will any blame or legal responsibility be held against the publisher or author, for any damages, reparation, or monetary loss due to the information contained within this book.Either directly or indirectly.

Legal Notice: This book is copyright protected. book is only for personal use. You cannot amend, distribute, sell, use, quote, or paraphrase any part, or the content within this book, without the consent of the author or publisher.

Disclaimer Notice: Please note the information contained within this document is for educational and entertainment purposes only. All effort has been executed to present accurate, up-to-date, and reliable, complete information. No warranties of any kind are declared or implied. Readers acknowledge that the author is not engaging in the rendering of legal, financial, medical or professional advice. The content within this book has been derived from various sources. Please consult a licensed professional before attempting any techniques outlined in this book. By reading this document, the reader agrees that under no circumstances are the author responsible for any losses, director indirect, which are incurred as a result of the use of information contained within this document, including, but not limited to, — errors, omissions, or inaccuracies.

Contents

Chapter 1
Introduction: Why Day Trading?

Chapter 2
How to Get the Most Out of This Book

Chapter 3
What Is Day Trading?

Chapter 4
Who Should Be Day Trading?

Chapter 5
Is It Possible to Make a Living As a Day Trader?

Chapter 6
How to Get Started Define Your Goals and Make a Plan

- 1.) Define Your SMART Goal
- 2.) Make a Plan
- 3.) Execute the Plan

Chapter 7: How Much Money Do You Need to Get Started?

Chapter 8
Determining Your Risk Tolerance

Chapter 9
What You Need to Begin Trading

- A Computer
- An Internet Connection
- A Charting Software
- eSignal (www.esignal.com)
- TradeStation (www.tradestation.com)
- MetaStock (www.metastock.com)
- Genesis Trade Navigator (www.genesisft.com)

- Trading Approaches
- The Right Concept for the Right Market

Chapter 10

How to Develop Your Own Profitable Day Trading Strategy

Step 1: Selecting a Market
- Trading Stocks
- A Little Bit of History
- A Little Bit of History

Step 2: Selecting a Timeframe

Step 3: Selecting a Trading Approach
- Fundamental Analysis
- Technical Analysis
- Trendline Validity

Step 4: Defining Entry Points

Step 5: Defining Exit Points
- Stop Losses
- Fixed Dollar Amount
- Percentage of the Current Price
- Percentage of the Volatility
- Using Technical Analysis
- Fixed Dollar Amount
- Percentage of the Current Price
- Percentage of the Volatility
- Using Technical Analysis

Step 6: Evaluating Your Strategy
- How to Read and Understand a Performance Report

- Total (Net) Profit
- Average Profit per Trade
- Winning Percentage
- Understanding Winning Percentage

Step 7: Improving Your Strategy

Chapter 11
The 10 Power Principles – Making Sure That Your Trading Plan Works
- Principle #1: Use Few Rules – Make It Easy to Understand
- Principle #2: Trade Electronic and Liquid Markets
- Principle #3: Have Realistic Expectations
- Principle #4: Maintain a Healthy Balance Between Risk and Reward
- Principle #5: Find a System That Produces at Least Five Trades per Week
- Principle #6: Start Small – Grow Big
- Principle #7: Automate Your Exits
- Principle #8: Have a High Percentage of Winning Trades
- Principle #9: Test Your Strategy on at Least 200 Trades
- Principle #10: Choose a Valid Back-Testing Period

Chapter 12
There's More To Trading Than Just Having a Strategy

Chapter 13
The Seven Mistakes of Traders and How to Avoid Them
- About Indicators

Chapter 14
The Trader's Psyche

Chapter 15
The Three "Secrets" to Day Trading Success

Chapter 1

Introduction: Why Day Trading?

If you're thinking about getting into day trading, then you've probably got a pretty strong motivation. More often than not, that motivation is money. You want to be rich. No, wait. Let me be a little more specific: you want to be wealthy.

Just to make sure that we're on the same page, let me touch on the vital difference between being "rich" and being "wealthy:"

>   1.) "Being rich" means that you have a lot of money.

>   2.) "Being wealthy" means that you have **time** to enjoy your money, time to do <u>what</u> you want to do <u>when</u> you want to do it.

So, is day trading the ultimate solution to becoming wealthy? Let's see.

Here's one way to become rich:
You work your way up to an executive position in a corporation and make hundreds of thousands of dollars a year. Of course, you'll be working at least 10 hours per day and at least six days per week.

Here are three ways to become wealthy:
  1.) Starting Your Own Company or Internet Business
  2.) Investing in Real Estate
  3.) Day Trading

Option 1: Starting Your Own Company or Internet Business

Having your own company means that you'll have to find or create a product, market the product, sell the product, deliver the product to your customers, and collect the payments.

These days, there are many "Internet Marketing Gurus" trying to sell you on the idea that you can automate everything, which will allow you to sleep late, do nothing, and cash very fat checks regularly. We both know that this is a dream, nothing more.

You can automate the routine, sure, but not the exceptions. And believe me: there are always exceptions when dealing with people – your customers. Plus, as long as you have computers involved, you need to keep Murphy's Law in mind: "Whatever can go wrong, WILL go wrong." Nothing could be more accurate!

Even if you *could* automate most of the delivery, you still have to find or create a product, set up a website, write a sales-copy, put the automation in place, and generate traffic. And since the Internet is evolving quickly, you will continuously update your website and traffic generation methods.

Okay, so what if you skipped the Internet part? Suppose you have a "physical" business. In that case, the headache might be even more significant: employees, vendors, lawyers, competitors, invoices, customers, production problems, office space, equipment, etc. I've known several small business owners who have given up and gotten a regular 9-5 job. Sometimes the reward isn't worth the stressful lifestyle.

Option 2: Investing In Real Estate:

Our second option on the road to wealth is investing in real estate. But with the market slowing down and the current credit crunch, it's not that easy anymore. Most lenders these days require a down payment of 1020% for investment properties, so you also need substantial capital to even get into the business.

Another problem is the cost of a transaction. Whenever you buy or sell a house, you will most likely have to pay a Realtor's commission and face closing costs. Because of these factors, it's not easy to quickly buy and sell houses. A transaction can last several days or several weeks. And on top of that, you always have the possibility of problems with renters (if you are renting out), or with contractors (if you are "fixin' and flippin'") or with legal issues if you use those "creative techniques" that some of the late-night infomercials are promoting. It boils down to one immense pain in the neck!

You need an appraisal, too, and you might have to argue with the appraiser about the value of the house; you need a home inspection and might be surprised when you learn of all the things that need to be fixed before you can sell; and, last but not least, your buyer might have to obtain a mortgage. As you know, the mortgage industry has become "interesting" in 2007 (to say the least). Buyers pre-approved and pre-qualified might learn the day before closing that they won't receive the promised loan. And all of these problems are just the tip of the iceberg. When it comes to hassle and problems, real estate investing is a flip of the coin, at best.
So, what's left?

Option 3: Day Trading
In my opinion, it's the perfect way to become wealthy. Here are ten reasons why:

> 1.) **It's the total "equal opportunity" job.**
>
>> Your race doesn't matter. Your skin color doesn't matter. Your education doesn't matter, whether you're a Ph.D. or a college drop-out. Your sex doesn't matter. Your origin doesn't matter. Your age doesn't matter. Your background and history don't matter. Even if you've been in jail for years, you could still make money with trading. Your language doesn't matter. Your looks don't matter. And your social status doesn't matter, as long as you

have sufficient funds to trade.

2.) **No employees to hire**

You don't have to hire any employees, which means you don't have to worry about job interviews, payroll, employee evaluations, holidays, sick days, or employee performance. Your only "team member" is your broker, and if he doesn't perform, ten others are waiting in line for your business.

3.) **No inventory, office space, or other equipment (besides your phone and your computer)**

You don't have to buy or rent expensive office space. You don't have to stock any products, which means you don't have to worry about expiration dates, damaged goods, shipping, handling, insurance, or displays and goods promotions.

4.) **No vendors, no customers, no invoices, and no accounts receivable**

You won't have to deal with any face-to-face contact. You don't need any vendors, you don't need to satisfy any customers, you don't need to provide any customer support, and you don't need to worry about any invoices, bounced checks, fraudulent credit card charges, returns, or charge-backs.

5.) **The time required is minimal.**

Whether you have a regular job or run your own business, the chances are that you're working at least 40 hours per week. With day trading, you can trade either part-time or full-time. You can start selling for as little as one hour per week, or you can go for a maximum of 2 hours per day.

It's your choice.

6.) Low capital requirement

You don't need a lot of money to get started. It is not like buying property, for example, where you're on the hook for a monthly mortgage and other cash-draining expenses. In trading, you can start with as little as $1,000! (We'll talk about how a little later.)

7.) Returns are almost instantaneous.

I'm talking "fast cash" in the sense that trading allows for quick liquidation. You can convert trades for cash within seconds. Where else in the world can you make money this fast and comfortably? You can buy and sell and buy again in minutes. You don't have to wait to see your profits. Try this with real estate or physical goods, where you might have to wait weeks or even months.

8.) Low transaction cost

You pay less than $10 per transaction in trading. Compare that to real estate transactions, in which you have to spend several thousand dollars in closing costs, not to mention a 3-6% commission to your realtor.

9.) It's simple to learn how to make money with day trading.

You don't have to go to college for years. And unlike most other professions, years of experience are not necessary either. After teaching hundreds of people how to make money with day trading, I firmly believe that <u>everybody</u> can learn how to become a successful trader.

10.) You don't need much to get started.

There are only six things that you DO need:
a.) A computer
b.) An Internet connection
c.) A charting software
d.) A broker
e.) An adequately funded trading account
f.) A good trading strategy

I could go on and on, but I think you get the picture. Throughout this book, we will cover much material that will help you get started with trading successfully. Here are a few of the essentials:

1.) What exactly is day trading
2.) Who should be day trading
3.) Is it possible to make a living as a day trader?
4.) What you need to get started
5.) How much money you'll need to begin trading
6.) What markets are out there, and which ones you should trade
7.) How to develop a profitable day trading strategy?
8.) How to ensure that your day trading strategy works

In short: you will learn everything you need to know to start making money with day trading. Ready?

****

Chapter 2

How to Get the Most Out of This Book

This book will help you become the trader you want to be, but it won't happen automatically. You will not instantly become successful the minute you finish reading.

Making money with day trading IS possible, but it requires time, discipline, effort, and commitment on your part.

Let me explain. Throughout the book, you'll learn key concepts that you can apply to your trading right away. The knowledge you accumulate is essential because it's what you base your trading decisions on, the decisions that will determine your ultimate success or failure.

One of my key goals in this book is to help you expand your trading knowledge to make well-informed decisions. I'll provide you with lots of valuable resources to help you learn what you need to know.

At the end of each chapter, you'll find **'Action Items,'** exercises relating to the topics recently covered. If you want to get the most out of this book, take a few minutes to complete these Action Items. The results you achieve will, in most cases, be directly proportional to the effort and commitment you invest in creating them.

I pledge to help you become the best trader that you can be, but I'll need your help to do it.

****

Chapter 3

What Is Day Trading?

Day trading is the practice of buying and selling financial instruments throughout the day. As the day progresses, prices will rise and fall in value, creating both the opportunity for gain and the possibility of loss.

At 10:15 am, a day trader might buy 1,000 shares of Amazon.com's stocks just as the price begins to rise on good news, and then sell it at 10:25 am, when it's up by $1 per share.

In this example, the day trader makes $1,000, minus commission. With today's cheap commissions of $10 or less per trade, that's a quick $990 in just 10 minutes!

When traded strategically, the markets' trends and fluctuations allow quick profits to be made briefly.

Keep in mind. However, that day trading is specifically designed to result in smaller earnings regularly; it is NOT intended to result in huge fortunes through a single trade.

Day trading can be very profitable, but it isn't a get-rich-quick scheme (though many seminars convincingly sell it as such). Nor is day trading a sure road to immeasurable wealth and success (as some hyped-up websites would have you believe).

Quite simply, day trading is just like any other business venture: to be successful at it, you need to have a PLAN. It would be very risky to dive in head-first without looking. However, with the right tools and the knowledge to use those tools efficiently and effectively – the risks of day trading can be significantly reduced. With perseverance and commitment, you CAN find trading success.

****

Chapter 4

Who Should Be Day Trading?

Day trading is not for everyone. Yes, there are many advantages, but there are also some "negative" factors. One of them is that you WILL face losses. As a trader, losses are part of our business. If you can't accept that fact, you simply shouldn't trade.

And you need a **PLAN**:
Traders who enjoy the most success in day trading, regardless of whether they're in it for a living or some extra income on the side, generally have concrete trading strategies and the discipline to stick to their trading plan.

Keep in mind that day trading is a very competitive field. To succeed, you need to maintain focus on a set of strategies that you can implement immediately, without hesitation. Remember, a proven, strategic trading plan can give you an edge over the rest of the market.

Unfortunately, even with a tested, proven trading strategy, you are not guaranteed trading success. It takes something else. It takes discipline.

A profitable strategy is useless without discipline. Successful day traders must have the field to follow their system rigorously because they know that only trades indicated by that system have the highest probability of resulting in a profit.

Whether you're new to trading or have been trading for years, it's all too tempting to place the entirety of your trust in graphs, charts, and software. If only trading was as easy as that!
Only purchasing trading templates and computer programs do not guarantee your success as a trader.

Too many hobby traders have tried that, and, unsurprisingly, they've failed. They bought the tools, but they didn't have the knowledge they needed to succeed. As in all things, education will do wonders for the aspiring – and experienced – trader.

Of course, this is not to say that software programs and markers are not helpful for day trading. On the contrary, many traders use technical indicators instrumental to their success – a few examples are the MACD, moving averages, and Stochastics. However, though profitable day traders DO follow their indicators, they are also aware that nothing is 100% foolproof.

You will not get wealthy on just a single trade.

Successful traders know that trying to hit a lucrative home run on just one trade is a sure way to get burned. The key is consistency. It would be best if you devised a solid strategy that produces consistent trading profits. You need to learn and adapt as your experience with day trading grows and evolves.

If you want to succeed with trading, you MUST invest both time and money to acquire the **knowledge** you need, the **discipline** to follow your trading strategy, and the **patience** to wait for the "perfect trade."

You need the following mindset:

1.) **Play Above the Line**

> Playing above the line means taking OWNERSHIP for everything that's happening in your trading. Rather than blaming, making excuses, or denying that there's a problem, be ACWho Should Be Day Trading?
> COUNTABLE for your trading decisions and actions, and take RESPONSIBILITY for doing something about it.

There is no "bad market," there's just a "bad trading approach to the market." Nobody forces you to trade a specific market. If a market becomes un-tradable, you can change to another market. And you can change your trading approach and adjust your trading plan. There are many things YOU can do. As a trader, YOU are responsible for your trading results, nobody else.

2.) Have a Positive Attitude

Trading can be simple, but it is not easy. You will face losses along the line, but you need to get up every morning believing in yourself, your strategy, and WINNING. Have you ever heard of "The Law of Attraction?" It states that to achieve success, you need to focus and concentrate on attaining that success. And the opposite applies too: if you focus on the negative – on losses – then you'll probably experience losses. It's essential that you ARE positive and that you STAY positive.

3.) Exercise Honesty

Did you overtrade this week? You let your emotions get the best of you? You didn't stick to the strategy? Fine – these things happen to the best of us. But don't lie to yourself, and don't make excuses. Take responsibility for your actions and your decisions.
Admit a mistake, learn from it, and move on.

4.) Be Committed

Trading success will not happen overnight. It requires commitment, time, and effort on your part. There are already too many "traders" in the market who think they know everything they need. They think they don't have to learn anything; they believe a "magic system" will place their trades for them and make them rich. You and I know that this is a sure path to failure.

Trading is like every other profession: you learn the basics, you apply them, you gain experience, and then you refine your trading. The learning never stops. Do you expect to make millions of dollars after only investing a few hours into your education? You wouldn't trust a doctor whose only education was from free, downloaded Internet eBooks, would you?

There's no doubt about it: day trading can be profitable and exciting to earn money. With the right knowledge, you can radically reduce the risk, which will create even more opportunities for achieving trading success.

Suppose you're not willing to spend the time learning the techniques of trading, reading about new and improved trading strategies, and working wholeheartedly in a fast-paced trading environment. In that case, day trading is probably not for you.

However, if you have the drive, dedication, and discipline, day trading could seriously impact your financial future's shape and success.

Action Items:

Decide right now that you will have the discipline to follow your plan, play above the line in your trading, maintain a positive attitude, exercise honesty, and be 100% committed to your trading success.

Start a trading journal. Most successful traders have one. Get your hands on a nice notebook and begin to record your trading progress and your feelings every day. You can start now. Write down today's resolutions; you will NOT use day trading to get rich quick. Circle it three times and read it frequently. It will help, trust me.

Trading for a Living

Before we get started, I need you to ask yourself one fundamental question: "How much is 'a living?'" Many people want to be 'rich,' but they fail to quantify what 'rich' means to them. Are you 'rich' if you have one million dollars?

Maybe so, but if you told Donald Trump that he had one million dollars in his bank account, he'd wonder what had happened to the rest of his money. He'd be furious! One million dollars to Donald Trump equals broke!

Over the past couple of years, I've taught

****

Chapter 5

Is It Possible to Make a Living As a Day Trader?

This question is asked over and over and over again by many, many people. The answer is: "Yes, it is possible!" And, better yet, you can do it.

Sometimes people don't believe me when I say that they can become successful, full-time day traders, but it's true. And I'm going to prove it to you right now.

Since I don't want to get into an in-depth discussion about "how much money is a decent living for *you*," let's just assume that you would be pretty happy if you were making $150,000 per year and let's say that you are making this money with your trading. Does that sound reasonable?

Let's break it down: $150,000 per year would be $12,500 per month, or if you prefer, $3,000 per week. It is assuming that you are taking two weeks of vacation per year.

IMPORTANT: Don't set daily targets when you trade. To make money, two conditions have to be met:

1.) **YOU** have to be ready to trade.
2.) **THE MARKET** must be ready to be traded.

There will be days when YOU are not at your best (sickness, emotional stress, no time because of an emergency, etc.). There will be days when the market is not ready to be traded (e.g., holidays, including the days before and after holidays, days before a major news release, like the Federal announcement regarding interest rates or the unemployment report, etc.).

Take a look at the following chart. The markets were open the day after

Thanksgiving and on Dec 24th and 26th. Still, there was barely anybody trading, which you can see reflected in the volume bars.

 It's the same between the rest of the days after Christmas and through New Year's Day in 2008. Though the markets were open, the volume was fragile. During these low-volume days, calls can be easily manipulated. They might behave very erratic, so it would be best to stay away from trading.

And that's why you shouldn't set daily goals in your trading: those goals will force you to trade on days when both of the previously mentioned conditions – you AND the market being ready – are NOT met.

It's important to start small and set a weekly goal for only ONE contract, or 100 shares. This goal should be LOW, shallow so that it is easy for you to reach it. Think about high-jumping: you train with a bar that's only three feet high. It's easy to jump. Then, once you manage three feet, you raise the bar another inch. And another. And another.

To trade successfully, you shouldn't raise the bar too high too fast. Put it at a level that you can manage every single time. You can always increase it at a later date once you've proven that you can meet your goal consistently.

Example:

In the first four weeks of your trading, you might set your weekly target at $100 per contract. It might sound too easy for you, but keep in mind that 90% of traders lose money in the markets. When you can make $100 per contract consistently, you can start "raising the bar." Try $150 per contract per week. Raise the bar repeatedly, but make sure that you're still comfortable achieving your goals.

When day trading futures, options, or forex, you can leverage and trade multiple contracts on a relatively small account. Suppose you're thinking about changing the futures market. In that case, you can easily find a broker who will enable you to trade one contract of almost any futures instrument that's out there – E-mini S&P, E-mini Russell, currency futures, interest rates, commodities, etc. – on a $2,000 account.

After a while, you might raise the bar to $300 per contract per week. If you want to make $3,000 per week, you need to trade ten contracts. The same applies to stock trading: if you can make $300 per week trading 100 shares, you need to sell 1,000 shares to make $3,000 per week.

At this point, you might not have enough money in your trading account to trade in these increments, but don't worry – we'll get there.

The critical element to trading success has a sound trading strategy that produces consistent profits. If you can make money day trading one contract or 100 shares of stock, you can make money day trading ten contracts or 1,000 shares.

Ideally, to achieve your weekly goal, you'll have a high average profit per trade. The average yield should be at least 50% higher than your average loss, preferably even twice as high.

One of the strategies that I use and teach to my students calls for a profit target of $300 per contract and a stop loss of $200 per contract. You'll notice that the profit target is greater than the stop loss. That's the beauty of it: all you need is one net winning trade, and you'll have achieved your weekly goal of making $300 per contract.

So if you're lucky, you could achieve your weekly profit target on Monday morning with the first trade.

But what if you lose?

As everyone in trading knows, losses are a part of the business, and you can't avoid them. If that's something you have trouble accepting, then you shouldn't be trading. However, there's a huge difference between losing big regularly and losing small in a controlled trading plan. You already know that you should keep your losses short; the key is to keep them smaller than your average wins.

Let's go back to the scenario I mentioned before: you have a trading strategy that produces $300 in profits for every win and costs you $200 for every loss. Now, if your weekly goal is $300, and if your first trade was a loss of $200, then you need to make two winning trades to achieve your weekly profit goal.

Let me take this a little further and break it down for you: you've lost $200 on your one losing trade, and then you make $600 on your two winning trades ($300 each). Your net profit = $400. Goal achieved. Now, STOP TRADING. Otherwise, you'll end up giving back the money you just made to the markets. Lock in your profits!

Of course, you're not always guaranteed a week with only one loss. Let's look at a week that starts with three losses. With three losses, you are now down $600 ($200 each). So you would need to have three wins that result in $900 ($300 each). Subtract the $600 you lost on the losing trades from the $900 you won on the winning trades, and your resulting net profit is $300. Goal achieved. Stop trading.

"Wait a minute – you're saying that I will achieve my goals with a winning percentage of only 50%?"

YES! That's what I'm saying! Read the example above again: you lost $600 on three losing trades, made $900 on three winning trades, and came out with a net profit of $300. It means that you could pick a losing trade every other time and STILL achieve your weekly profit goals!

I want to stress this point again because many traders neglect this vital concept of setting weekly goals. They define daily goals, which create an enormous psychological pressure, and then they trade markets when they shouldn't, and they lose.

So let's just assume for a minute that you do end up achieving an actual winning percentage of only 50%. Now, when you start trading again on Monday morning, what are your chances of having a winning trade? 50%! You have a one in two chance of meeting your weekly profit goal in just one single vocation!

So if you DO achieve your weekly profit goal on the first trade Monday morning, what next?

Stop trading for that week! Just enjoy life! It doesn't get any better than that.

Remember, you need to stick to your trading plan and your weekly goal. Do NOT enter into another trade once you've already achieved your weekly goal; the chance that your second trade may be a losing trade is too great, and you would be giving your money and profits back to the market. Overtrading and greediness are a trader's downfall, so resist them and stick to your strategies.

Now, you know that you can achieve your weekly profit goal with a winning percentage of only 50%. Throughout this book, I will help you get an even sharper edge in your trading, creating a trading strategy with an even higher winning percentage.

A Quick Recap:

The first step towards financial success is to define your weekly profit target. Next, you need to find a reliable, straightforward trading strategy to help you achieve your profit goal. When you enter into a trade and your trade hits either your profit target OR your stop loss, exit that work immediately. Stick to your trading plans and strategies until you achieve your weekly profit goal, and then give yourself rest until next week.

If you think back to the case I gave at the beginning of this section, to make $150,000 per year – assuming a 50-week year and two weeks of vacation – you'd need to make $3,000 per week. At a $300 profit per trade, this means that you would need to trade ten contracts (or 1,000 shares). Of course, this illustration can be applied to various amounts. If you wanted to make $225,000 per year with a weekly profit target of $300 per contract, for example, then you would have to trade 15 deals (or 1,500 shares), and so on, and so on.

If you don't have a trading account that lets you trade the number of contracts or shares that I'm talking about yet, then now is the perfect time to start building it. Remember, be patient with your trading, be smart, be slow, and be steady. Trading success doesn't happen overnight, but you can achieve profitable results in a much shorter period than you may have thought possible with the right strategies and structure.

Plan your trades and trade your plan.
THAT'S how successful traders make money.
Action Items:

Start your trading plan now. You will find a trading plan template in the appendix on page 245. Define how much money is "making a living" for you.

How much money do you want to make with trading? Break down your overall goals into monthly and weekly targets.
****

Chapter 6

How to Get Started Define Your Goals and Make a Plan

When it comes to trading, many first time traders want to jump right in with both feet. Unfortunately, very few of those traders are successful; successful trading requires knowledge, skill, and experience.

Before you dive in, you need to determine what your goals are. What do you hope to achieve with your trading activities? Why do you want to trade?

1.) To buy a new sports car?
2.) To buy a bigger house?
3.) To make $100,000 a year / month / week?
4.) To finance a college education for your children?
5.) To make a full-time income to support your entire family?
6.) Freedom to choose what, when, and who you do things with?
7.) To have a fun, exciting life full of extraordinary experiences?
8.) To work less and enjoy more time with your loved ones?
9.) Or are you just planning to make some extra cash on weekends?

Before you trade a single penny, really think about what you hope to achieve with that investment. Knowing your goal will help you stay motivated when you're facing a severe spell of trading, and it'll help you make smarter investment decisions along the way.

But be realistic:

Too often, people start day trading with dreams of becoming rich overnight. I'm not going to say that it is impossible (because it is possible), but let me remind you that it's also scarce. It's much safer to create a trading strategy that will allow your account to grow at a slower pace over time, which can ultimately be used for retirement or a child's education.

Let's talk about defining your goals and making a plan for your day trading endeavors.

Here are the three essential steps:

1.) Define Your SMART Goal

SMART is an acronym that stands for:

1.) **S**pecific
2.) **M**easurable
3.) **A**ttractive
4.) **R**ealistic
5.) **T**imeframe

Fortunately, it's straightforward to define a goal that meets all of these criteria for day trading. You specify exactly how much money you would like to make per month with your day trading.

Example:

I want to make $10,000 per month with day trading.

- **Is this SPECIFIC?** – Yes, a dollar amount of $10,000 in particular.

- **Is this MEASURABLE?** – Absolutely! Just check the balance of your trading account at the beginning of the month and the end of the month. Your account balance is the easiest way to measure the achievement of your goal.

- **Is this ATTRACTIVE?** – That depends on you. $10,000 is attractive for someone who currently makes $4,000 per month, but it wouldn't be appealing to someone who's already paying $10,000 just in mortgage payments for his 6,000 square foot home. Make sure that YOU are motivated by this goal.

- **Is this REALISTIC?** – We talked about this in the previous chapter. Successful people believe that there are no unrealistic goals, only unrealistic timeframes. Right now, your trading account may not be big enough for you to realistically trade enough shares or contracts to achieve your long-term trading goal. Still, if you follow the steps outlined in this book, your long-term goal may become realistic shortly.

- **Does it have a TIMEFRAME?** – Of course, it does: you want to make $10,000 per month; the timeframe is 30 days.

2.) Make a Plan

Developing a plan is essential to your success, but we're getting a little ahead of ourselves. We'll talk about your trading plan in detail in the second part of the book, "Your Trading Strategy – The Cornerstone to Your Trading Success." Just make sure you don't mix up the order: you <u>first</u> define your trading goals and develop a trading plan.

Many traders look for a trading strategy first and then hope that the trading strategy will help them achieve their goals. That's putting the cart in front of the horse.

Regardless of what you're doing, you should first define WHAT you want to accomplish and then plan HOW to achieve that goal. Otherwise, you might find out that you started climbing up the wrong ladder right at the very beginning.

3.) Execute the Plan

It is where the rubber meets the road. Once you have your plan, you'll need to execute it. And naturally, that's where most of us fail.

Let me give you an example:

Amazon lists 18,361 books for "Weight Loss" and another 28,707 readers for "Exercising and Fitness." That's a total of 47,068 books on the popular topic "How to Lose Weight" (compared to only 4,463 books in the category "Stock Trading and Investing").

If I wrote a book on weight loss, it would be very, very short:

1.) Eat less.
2.) Exercise more.

Come on. It's simple: we all know that we can lose 10 pounds in 10 weeks if we just follow those two rules.

We reduce our calorie intake to 1,500 or 2,000 calories per day. Then we do some aerobic exercises at least three times a week for a minimum of 30 minutes.

We have a SMART goal ("lose 10 pounds in 10 weeks"), and we have a plan ("eat less and exercise more"), so why do we keep buying these books and magazines that promise a new diet, a new way to lose weight?

Because we fail to execute our plan, and then we blame the project: "it's too hard," "it's impossible," "it doesn't work." It isn't true. We failed because we were too lazy or didn't have the discipline to execute our plan. But instead of working on the real problem – the execution – we change the program itself, hoping that there's an easier way.

Successful people will realize that their problem doesn't lie in the plan but the execution. Here's what you can do to ensure your motivation and discipline when it comes to executing your plan:

It's essential to focus on the big picture. It'll help you stay motivated when your learning reaches a plateau or when you face a couple of losses. All significant accomplishments start with a great vision.

Once you've defined your SMART goal and the amount of money you want to make with trading, ask yourself this: "How would achieving this goal impact your family life?" and "how would it affect you personally?"

Take your time to answer these questions and write down the answers. As you know, human beings are great at procrastination. We don't like to be outside of our comfort zone, and that's why sometimes we do nothing and just "hope" that we will achieve our goals. As you can imagine, the chances of achieving a goal by doing nothing are slim to none. So, answering the next question will help you to take action immediately.

Ask yourself: "Why should you act NOW?" When you take the time to think about the answer, it will be a huge motivator. Little tricks like this will help you stay focused on your long-term goal, helping you execute your plan.

Action Items:

> Continue your trading journal. Write down WHY you want to trade and what you are trying to accomplish with your trading. Be specific! Define your smart goals. Dream big.

Write down the impact that your trading success will have on YOUR life and the life of your family. It is an essential step because it'll help you get through the challenging times, which all traders experience.

****

Chapter 7: How Much Money Do You Need to Get Started?

The answer to that question depends on the market you want to trade. Using a systematic approach, we'll determine the best need for you throughout the next few chapters, but the information below will give you a basic idea of your options:

1.) If you want to day trade stocks, you need at least $25,000 in your trading account.

2.) If you want to day trade futures, you should have between $5,000 and $10,000 in your trading account.

3.) When trading options, you should have between $1,000 and $5,000 in your trading account.

4.) If you're thinking about trading forex, then you can start with as little as $500 in your trading account.

Financial considerations are always important but don't make the common mistake of letting your current financial situation dictate which market you're going to trade.

Remember: you <u>first</u> define your goal, and <u>then</u> you plan how to achieve it.

If you don't have sufficient funds to trade the markets you've outlined in your goals, then start doing something about it now – save more money or put in overtime hours. There are many ways to make a few more bucks, and it's better to wait for the funds you need than to begin trading in a market that isn't right for you and your goals.

For those of you who already have the right amount of money in your savings account, let's talk about the question, **"How much money SHOULD you trade?"**

Many first-time traders think they should trade all of their savings. It isn't true! To determine how much money you should exchange, you must first determine how much you can afford to lose your financial goals.

Let's begin by determining how much of your savings should remain in your savings account. It's important to keep three to six months of living expenses in a readily accessible savings account, so set that money aside, and don't trade it! You should never exchange money that you may need immediately. Unless you have funds from another source, such as a recent inheritance, the remaining amount of money will probably be what you currently have to trade with.

Take a good look at how much money you can currently afford to trade. You don't want other parts of your life to suffer when you tie your money up in a trade, so make sure to consider what these savings were initially for.

Next, determine how much you can add to your trading activities in the future. If you are currently employed, you will continue to receive an income, and you can plan to use a portion of that income to build your investment portfolio over time.

Two more important things to remember:

1.) As outlined above, certain types of investments require an initial deposit amount to get started. It does not mean that you will be risking the whole amount (see the chapter "Determining Your Risk Tolerance" on page 27). Many traders are only willing to bet 10% of the initial deposit.
2.) Never borrow money to trade, and never use money that you can't afford to lose!

Action Items:

Take a financial inventory. Considering the points mentioned above, define how much money you have to trade with right now.

If you don't have enough money to start trading yet, make a plan to save or earn the money you still need.

****

Chapter 8

Determining Your Risk Tolerance

Each individual has a risk tolerance that should not be ignored. Any good broker or financial educator knows this, and they can help you determine what your risk tolerance is and work with you to find investments that do not exceed that risk tolerance.

Determining one's risk tolerance involves several different things. First off, you need to know how much money you have to invest and your investment and financial goals.

For instance, if you plan on retiring in ten years and haven't saved a single penny yet, you'll need to have a high-risk tolerance because you'll need to do some aggressive trading to reach your financial goal.

On the other side of the coin, if you're in your early twenties and want to start investing for your retirement, your risk tolerance can be below. You can afford to watch your money grow slowly over time.

Of course, you realize that your need for a high-risk tolerance or your need for a low-risk tolerance has no bearing on how you feel about risk. Again, there is a lot in determining your tolerance.

For instance, if you entered a trade and see that transaction go against you, what would you do?

Let's say you are facing a $100 loss. Would you sell out, or would you stay in the trade? If you have a low tolerance for risk, you would want to sell out. If you have a high tolerance, you would wait and see what happens.

This decision is not based on what your financial goals are. This tolerance is based on how you feel about your money.

And, of course, your account size plays a vital role in determining your risk tolerance. If you have a $2,000 account, then a $1,000 loss might make you nervous since you are losing 50% of your capital.

But if your trading account size is $100,000, and you are facing a $1,000 loss, then you might be more relaxed since it is only 1% of your account.

As you'll learn, emotions are a significant factor in trading; therefore, it's essential to take the time to determine your risk tolerance. Talk to a professional if needed. A good trading coach, financial advisor, or broker should help you choose the level of risk you are comfortable with.

Action Items:

> Determine your risk tolerance. If you're unsure about how to go about doing this, get in contact with my company, Rockwell Trading®, and we'll provide you with a set of questions that will help you determine your risk tolerance.

****

Chapter 9

What You Need to Begin Trading

Today trade, you'll need:
- 1.) A computer
- 2.) An Internet connection
- 3.) A charting software
- 4.) A broker
- 5.) An adequately funded trading account
- 6.) A good trading strategy

A Computer

You don't need the latest computer, and you don't need the most expensive one. Any computer that you've purchased in the past two years will do the trick. Most charting software and trading platforms run on Windows, so if you're thinking about getting a MAC, make sure that the software you are considering is MAC compatible. Notebooks are fine, too. Just as a guideline, here are the minimum specifications:

- 1.) IBM or IBM compatible Pentium IV-class computer
- 2.) 1 GHz or greater
- 3.) Windows 2000, Windows XP
- 4.) 256MB RAM (use 1GB of RAM when running Windows XP)
- 5.) CD-ROM drive
- 6.) Minimum of 3GB of hard disk space

You'll also need a second screen. You should have your charting software on ONE screen for the entry and exit signals and your trading platform on the ANOTHER screen to enter the orders. A second monitor will cost you around $150-$250. Don't be cheap on monitors; you need to ensure that you can see your charting software in crystal-clear clarity. A 17" monitor will do the trick. A 19" is even better. Over 19" is pretty much overkill. You can have a bigger monitor, but you don't need one.

An Internet Connection

Don't be cheap here. Don't ever try to trade using dial-up or a modem connected to your phone. A reliable Internet connection is essential for your trading success. After all, the data you receive from the market is what you'll base ALL of your trading decisions upon, so you can't afford a delay.

Invest in a DSL or cable connection. No T1 connection is needed.

A Charting Software

Online day trading has developed to the point where charting software is an indispensable tool for both professional and novice-day traders. The times when you drew your charts in a notebook using quotes from the morning newspaper are long gone. These days, powerful charting software packages allow you to access the market information in real-time; this information is displayed in various ways, all of which can help you carry out your trades.

Choosing the "right" charting software is a very personal decision – it can be compared to selecting the right car. What another trader chooses may be different from what you choose, and vice versa. That's why it's essential for you to carefully evaluate a list of features – with both advantages and disadvantages – before deciding on a data feed and charting package.

The bottom line is that you need to have a list of criteria, and you need to compare and contrast the available charting packages using that list. Make your choice based on the results. Here are some examples of criteria you may want to use:

- **Real-Time Data**

    You need a stable platform that can deliver real-time data instantly. This feature alone will exclude many of the options available because many web-based programs will have some sort of delay. When it comes to day trading and swing trading, you can't afford to deal with uncertainty, even if that delay would be perfectly acceptable in long-term trading.

- **Market Data Coverage**

Check out the markets that are covered by the charting software. Most packages include the major U.S. markets, but if you need other international markets, like Asian or European markets, then you need to make sure that data is available in real-time.

- **Wide Variety of Indicators**

Depending on your individual needs, you might be interested in a broad range of indicators and charting methods, such as bar charts, point-and-figure charting, or Japanese candlesticks. Besides, check to see if the charting software can quickly display fundamental indicators like MACD, RSI, and Moving Averages. If you're serious about technical analysis, make sure that you can program your hands or modify the existing ones to your needs without too much hassle.

- **Competitive Rates & Money Back Guarantee**

You need trading software that will not cost you all of your money before you even enter your first trade. It's essential to shop around. However, finding a competitive rate does not mean that the provider's software is the cheapest. You have to be careful on this one – the old saying "you get what you pay for" definitely applies to trading. Weigh your options. You don't want cheap trading software that offers you next to nothing, but you probably don't need the most expensive package – with features you won't even use – either.

Ensure that the provider you select will allow time for you to test how the software platform works. If you're uncomfortable with using it, you should be able to claim a refund within the first 30 days.

- **User-Friendly Platform & Complete Training**

    Unless you're a skilled computer programmer, you need to have a platform that you can use easily, not one that requires a degree as a Computer Engineer. Trust me, those types of media ARE out there! You'll need software that allows you to back-test strategies and program custom indicators and trading systems without a lot of trouble.

    And, if you just can't seem to find trading software out there that is EASY to use, then find a software platform that comes with a detailed user guide. A guide will help you become familiar with the system and educate you at the same time.

- **Reputable Company**

    Choose a reputable company that has an established presence on the Internet for its platform and data feed. And naturally, choose a company that has excellent customer support service.

    Keep in mind that you can add other criteria to this list based on your trading goals, such as the ability to switch between different timeframes quickly. As I said previously: it's a very personal choice that only you can make.

The following section includes my reviews of a few major software packages.

eSignal (www.esignal.com)

Interactive Data Corporation owns eSignal, and it's been around in the trading industry for more than 20 years. In April 1999, it was launched on the Internet.

As of February 2008, the prices for eSignal range from $125/month (for eSignal Premier) to $195/month (for eSignal Premier Plus), which makes this package slightly more expensive than several other trading platforms out there. If you're an options trader, you'll have the capability to see 1,000 symbols through an options analysis package. In other words, you can expect to pay as much as $249 to $360 every month.

However, given that eSignal's charting and data feeds are coming from the same provider, there will be no issues that the software provider can blame on the data feed or vice versa. (This "blame game" is something that every professional trader has – or will – experience at some point while using trading software).

In my opinion, eSignal's user interface is not the most intuitive available on the market today; it's often necessary for users to refer to the help system over and over again. However, the charts can be customized in many different ways, according to your needs. Once you get used to the various shortcuts, the charting platform is pretty useful for fast decision-making.

When it comes to a tutorial system, the company provides complete audio and video training to new users. There's no need to fear being a newbie – you can familiarize yourself with the software in no time.

Now, after you set up a chart in a way that you're comfortable with – which is done by customizing sizes, colors, indicators, etc. – you can save this format and apply it to other charts without delay. The sets of maps and quote lists can be saved as 'Pages,' and it's possible to swiftly and efficiently switch between these pages.

Every window in the platform can be popped out of the main eSignal window, which helps get the best out of that multi-monitor system of yours. Besides the charts, eSignal offers quote lists, level 2 screens, and news tickers to keep you updated. All of these features can be connected. For example, picking a symbol in a quote list will make all of the linked charts, level 2 screens, etc., change to the same symbol almost immediately.

All of the standard technical indicators are available. There's also a program using JavaScript language called EFS (which is the foundation language for eSignal Formula Script) for writing your series of procedures; these procedures can be employed repeatedly throughout the programs' lives. EFS can also be used for communicating with broker interfaces and, of course, for back-testing.

If you want to get into more advanced customization, there are a couple of API levels offered at additional cost, and these supply raw access to the eSignal data feed. A standard subscription will let you monitor up to 100 symbols, the next level up being 250, and if that's not enough, you can pay a little extra to get even more characters to monitor.

The data feed itself is probably the best ingredient of the eSignal package. A trustworthy global market data feed, which eSignal has staked its well-known reputation in the active trader community on, is available right in front of you. To guarantee a nonstop transmission and perfect data accuracy, the company maintains fully redundant ticker plants, and data can be exported through a flat-file for you to open in Excel or another spreadsheet application.

eSignal is, without a doubt, one of the best data feeds you can find on the Internet. The charting product is powerful enough for most traders, with EFS adding to its effectiveness.

TradeStation (www.tradestation.com)

Since it arrived in the online trading community in 1997, TradeStation has become the top choice for tens of thousands of high-rated traders worldwide; it's won various awards from industry publications, including Barron's and Technical Analysis of Stocks and Commodities. It was also named Stocks and Commodities Magazine's Reader's Choice Award for Best Trading

Software five years in a row, from 1994 to 1999. It is generally accepted as the industry standard when it comes to chart software.

TradeStation is probably the first trading platform in the world that gives you the ability to create, test, and fully automate your rule-based trading strategies daily. When you're ready for your first trade, TradeStation can watch your trading rules and even carry out your transactions 100% automatically.

It's also designed to help you discover some potential market opportunities and then perform your trades more professionally than you could ever do on your own. TradeStation essentially monitors the markets for you tick by tick, in real-time on the Internet, and seeks out all of the opportunities based on your trading plans.

The instant an opportunity arises based on your custom buy or sell rules. It's designed to automatically generate your entry and exit orders and send them to the marketplace within fractions of a second of the market move.

TradeStation even created a programming language called EasyLanguage that is very user friendly once you get its hang. You can easily create your own trading rules, such as when to enter the market and buy or when to get out and sell. You can automate practically all of the trading strategies you could ever think of, including multiple orders, entries and exits, profit targets, protective stops, trailing stops, and more.

It allows you to back-test, program custom indicators, and modifies indicators to your needs. Then, with just a single click of your mouse, it will back-test your strategy on up to 20 years of accurate, intra-day market data, giving you the simulated results. TradeStation will provide you with information on all of the trades you would have positioned, your simulated net profit or losses, and much more before you even risk one single penny from your real trading funds.

When you first set up TradeStation, it may be a little overwhelming for you to use the software. However, for $99.95 to $199.95/month, which allows you to utilize TradeStation's award-winning features, it is probably worth your time to become skilled and get acquainted with this trading platform.

It is no coincidence that TradeStation has become one of the most desirable trading platforms for active traders, both professionals, and novices, through its dependability and the power of automation.

MetaStock (www.metastock.com)

If you love using the technical analysis strategy, MetaStock by Equis International (Reuters have acquired Equis) might be your #1 tool to trade. And, if you don't know anything about technical analysis, but you've always wanted to apply this kind of approach when it comes to your investments, then you might be interested in using this software as a learning tool.

As of February 2008, MetaStock is available for a one-time fee of $1,395.

You can use QuoteCenter, which receives real-time data directly from Reuters – the leading source of financial news to the world's media – and combine it with MetaStock Pro. The main program itself is very user friendly, and it's relatively easy to familiarize yourself with all of its functions, even if you're a beginner. The program is also fully compatible with Microsoft Office, which means you can directly cut and paste data into Excel or Word.

Equis has provided all types of chart forms and features; trendlines, moving averages, resistance lines, support lines, and various other trade tools are accessible by simply clicking and dragging your mouse. You can also choose the Internet option to receive quotes, news, and option symbols straight from Reuters, without any charge.

The new version, MetaStock Professional 8, includes all of the previous version's capabilities – such as extensive charting and analysis – and it's designed to work with a real-time data feed such as BMI or Signal Online from the Data Broadcasting Corporation.

Many traders say that one of the best features in Metastock is the search facility. The search facility will let you search your entire database of stocks and shares based on your specified criteria. The plan is to uncover any stocks that display according to your trading strategy. The program will then calculate how much money you could make using a particular trading strategy. The results will give you detailed information, such as when to buy and sell at what price and how much was made or lost from each trade.

Equis will also give you a CD full of historical data from which you can create charts, along with the online connection you need to upgrade the database anytime you want. You'll receive a 550-page manual of Technical Analysis, from A to Z, which will make even the novice trader able to master the software and technical analysis methods in no time. Not to mention that the 'HELP' menu even includes an interactive visual tutorial so that you won't get bored.

Genesis Trade Navigator (www.genesisft.com)

Trade Navigator, the trading platform designed by Genesis Financial Technologies, Inc., is a sophisticated charting, technical analysis, and execution platform. Used in conjunction with many trading strategies, Trade Navigator can turn into a perfect, real-time automated trading instrument, using indicators like Moving Averages, Seasonal, ADX, and Stochastics. Functions such as Single-Click Trading, Calendar, Indicator, Bracketing, Trailing Stop, and more are available right at your fingertips.

OHLC, Candlestick, Line, Mountain, HLC, HL, Histograms, and Points are also included in the platform, and the charts can be separated into panes. Panes can hold any single Indicator or Study, or even a mixture of the two, allowing you to customize the way each chart looks by simply clicking and dragging your mouse to draw, resize, move, or expand the trendlines, support and resistance lines, and other objects. Therefore, no matter what kind of display options you want to employ, Trade Navigator is the ideal tool for you.

The Trade Navigator Platinum can do all of the back-testing, developing, and analyzing your trading strategies utilizing Tradesense. This simple input language does not require you to be an expert in computer science to use it. It comes with a complete training video series, free training, and a manual. Tradesense is the core feature of the Platinum system, and you can learn it pretty fast. It combines everyday English and simple math symbols for robust analytics and crucial input.

With Tradesense, you can take any strategy idea – whether from a trading book, a seminar, or even from your friend – and test it using various order types (such as limit orders and stop orders) to develop and analyze its performance. Tradesense will spot the indicators you're looking for and then automatically fill in the values for you.

Precision Tick is another unique feature from the Genesis testing system; it allows you to back-test any strategy. It ensures that every rule is executed precisely based on real-time market conditions. You also can create your next bar orders. Any process you put into the program can be completed with an "Action." Once specific criteria are met, whether Long or Short, it will let you place a given order.

With Trade Navigator, you can create your custom indicators and strategies, you can trade directly from the chart, and you can use the Instant Replay mode if you want to practice your trading. Speaking of which, with Instant Replay, you can go back to a specific date in the past and observe the data as it fills in, watching how it moves on the days that the bars were created.

It's like having your time machine, which allows you to travel back in time and then move forward to the present time as you watch the chart changing in front of your eyes. Instant Replay mode is the perfect tool for any type of trader to plan for real-time trading without any risk at all.

Trade Navigator is available in three different versions: Silver, Gold, and Platinum. Prices start at $99 plus data updating fees of $25 per month for stocks, or you can pick the package of $65 per month for stocks, futures, indexes, and some options. To help you run the software immediately, Genesis allows you to use hundreds of pre-programmed indicators and parameters so that you'll be able to identify the best strategy based on your approach quickly.

Genesis also has various training videos available and offers free webinars regularly to help you get the most out of their software package.

Charting Software Conclusion

Hopefully, you now have a better idea of what type of trading software will best fulfill your needs. Remember, powerful charting software is what gives you the velocity and ability to carry out nearly instantaneous trades in response to breaking news. In time, you might want to move on to more sophisticated software as you become more experienced in the trading world.

Remember, don't purchase trading software before you compare all of the packages available. If you don't take the time to compare and contrast, you may get sucked into cheap software that doesn't have the functions you need; OR, you may get suckered into expensive software that has many features that you'll never use.

If you need any help setting up your trading platform or have any other questions, you can always utilize the company's customer support.

Take advantage of free trials and money-back guarantees. Remember, selecting the right software for you is a very personal choice, and you won't know if it's right for you until you test-drive it.

A Broker

You may wonder if you need a broker. The answer is yes. If you intend to day trade, then you must have a broker. And it doesn't matter whether you are trading stocks, futures, forex, or options: unless you are a member of the exchange, you won't be able to place your orders without a broker.

Stock-, futures-, and options-brokers are required to pass different tests to obtain their licenses. These tests ensure that the broker knows his business and will be able to support you if needed.

It's essential to understand the difference between a broker and a market analyst. An analyst analyzes the stock or futures market, predicting what it will or will not do or how specific stocks or commodities might perform. A broker is there to follow your instructions to either buy or sell, not to analyze the markets.

In most cases, brokers earn their money from commissions on sales. When you instruct your broker to buy or sell, they make a set percentage of the transaction. Many brokers charge a flat 'per transaction' fee.

There are two types of brokers: **full-service brokers** and **discount brokers**.

Full-service brokers can usually offer more types of investments, provide you with investment advice, and are typically paid in commissions.

Discount brokers typically do not offer any advice or research; they do as you ask them to do, without all of the bells and whistles.

So, the most significant decision you must make when it comes to brokers is whether you want a full-service broker or a discount broker.

If you are new to investing, you may need to go with a full-service broker to ensure that you are making wise investments. They can offer you the skills that you lack at this point. However, if you are already knowledgeable about the market you want to trade, then all you need is a discount broker to make your trades for you.

Selecting the right broker can be a tedious battle for most novice traders. There are more than a hundred online brokers today, and additional choices are becoming available all the time.

The challenge lies with too many choices – it isn't easy to choose which broker is best for you amongst all of the many options out there.

This section, though, is all about providing you with some essential tips for picking an ideal trading broker.

First off, you'll need to double your diligence if you're looking for a forex trading broker. Since the foreign exchange market is worth trillions of dollars, it offers lucrative opportunities for brokers to set up their firms online. And since the foreign exchange market is decentralized, it can be hard to identify quality brokers amongst all of the unscrupulous brokers with fraudulent practices.

Your chances of finding an honest and reliable forex trading broker will dramatically increase if you follow the guidelines below:

- Always request references that you can speak with.

- Do a check with the local regulatory agencies and make sure that the forex trading broker is registered. For U.S.-based brokers, see if they are registered as Futures Commission Merchants (FCM) with the Commodity Futures Trading Commission (CFTC) and registered with the National Futures Association (NFA).

- Compare the account details, such as the minimum deposit required, leverage, spreads, and so on. Ask them specifically if commissions are chargeable, lot fees, etc. It is to ensure that you do not incur hidden costs. Some sneaky brokers will deliberately give you an impression that they are the cheapest to use, but in fact, they'll hit you where it hurts when it comes to hidden charges.

- The trading platform needs to be user-friendly. Many traders, especially first-timers, find it challenging to navigate trading software. Just making sense of the charts and currency prices can be a challenge. So, if there are demo accounts, try them.

I've also included a list of questions for you to ask your broker in the appendices.

Remember, this broker or brokerage will be your teammate when it comes to making you a wealthy person. So be picky and be cautious.

A Properly Funded Trading Account

You need money to trade. But you've also heard this warning several times: "Don't trade with money that you can't afford to lose." You might think this is just the typical disclaimer that every professional in the trading industry has to use. But it's not. It's much more.

Let me give you an example:

A few weeks ago, I received an email from a trader who told me that his wife had given him a deadline: if he were not trading profitably within the next four weeks, he would have to stop selling altogether and get a 'real job.'

I'm not saying that this trader's wife didn't have ground to stand on, but, as you'll learn in the third part of this book, there's more to trading than just having a strategy. You might have heard that a trader's two biggest enemies are fear and greed. It is very often the case. That's why controlling your emotions is extremely important to your trading.

Now, imagine this trader's situation for me. He MUST be profitable every single week for the next four weeks. Do you think he will be calm and relaxed when he enters a trade? Do you think he will be in control of his emotions? If he loses a few exchanges, do you think he'll stick to his trading strategy and plan?

Or do you think he'll be afraid of losing money, which means having to give up what he LOVES to do? It will probably be hard to stick to a plan or strategy if he gets hit with more and more losses. Don't you think it's pretty likely that he'll start making bad decisions and begin, in essence, to gamble his money in the markets, hoping for wins?

I can't stress enough how important it is not to pressure yourself or your trading performance. And to keep the pressure to a minimum, you probably shouldn't quit your day job just yet. Before becoming a professional day trader, your trading must be consistent, and your profits should be almost predictable. Give yourself some time to prove that you have what it takes to trade for a living.

As to the amount of money you need, that depends on you. Having too much money in your trading account can be just as dangerous as having too little. If you have $100,000 in your trading account and only risk $100 per trade, you might think of your losses as 'peanuts.' Even though we must learn to accept failures as a part of the business, we should still never think of them as 'peanuts!' There is a balance. You have to find it.

So, to avoid situations like the afore-mentioned trader got himself into, fund your account appropriately – not too much and not too little. And be prepared for a time where you may not make a lot of money with it. As with everything, there is a learning process when it comes to trading.

For more information on the right amount of money to get started with, see the chapter "How Much Money Do You Need to Get Started?" on page 23.

A Trading Strategy

Last but not least: you need a trading strategy.

You can have the latest computer, six screens, a T1-Internet connection, the best broker in the world, and a well-funded trading account, but none of these will produce trading profits for you.

NEVER start trading without a trading strategy.

In the next part of this book, you'll learn how to develop a profitable trading strategy that works for you.

Action Items:

> Check your computer to see if it fulfills the minimum requirements outlined in this chapter. If not, determine how much it will cost to upgrade your computer. You do not have to upgrade your computer – or buy a new one – now, but you should know the cost if you're getting ready to trade.
>
> Check your current Internet connection and determine the cost for an upgrade if needed. Same as with the other trading elements: there's no need to upgrade now, but you'll want to know the cost once you start your trading business.
>
> Take a look at different charting software packages. Most of them offer a free 30-day trial. Get familiar with the software and decide based on the "ease of use" of the software, NOT on the price. You'll work with this software almost every day, so it's essential to choose one that fits YOU best. When you start your trading career, you don't want to spend a lot of time learning the software. It should be intuitive and easy-to-use.

Start calling several brokers to obtain quotes. The brokerage business is highly competitive, so you need to shop around for the best commission. But, as outlined above: do NOT base your decision purely on commissions. Your broker is your only team member, and you want to have a team member you trust and who knows you. Try to find a "personal broker" who has a direct line and doesn't "hide" in a call center. Ask him what he can offer you. After a few calls, you will get the feeling of a "good" broker.

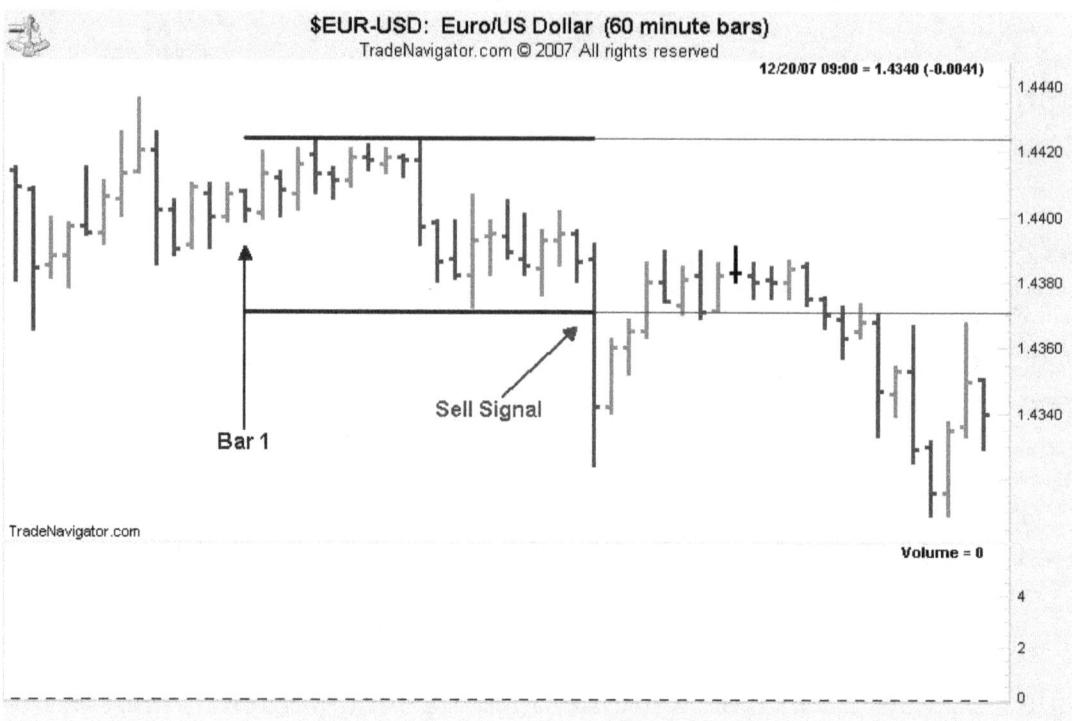

Prices moved below the 20-bar low at 1.4372 and generated a short signal. Prices moved as low as 1.4324 (= 48 pips or $480) before retracing.

Please note that we just defined an entry signal. You still need to apply profit targets and stop losses (see the next two chapters).

Moving Average Convergence Divergence (MACD)

Another trend-following indicator is the Moving Average Convergence/Divergence (MACD), developed by Gerald Appel. It indicator shows the relationship between two moving averages of prices. The most popular parameter for the MACD is the difference between a 26-bar exponential moving average (EMA) and the 12-bar. Its difference is then plotted on the chart and oscillates above and below zero.

A 9-bar EMA of the MACD called the "signal line" is then plotted on top of the MACD, functioning as a trigger for buy and sell signals (dark gray line).

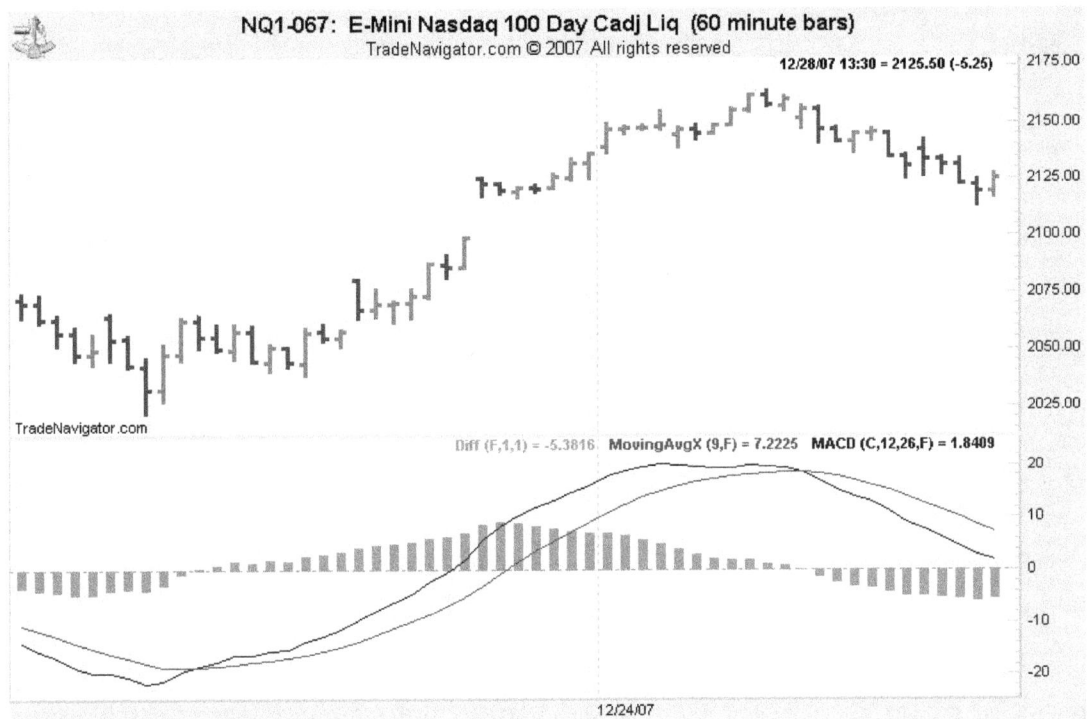

Traders utilize the MACD in different ways, but the most popular is to use the signal line for entry signals:

- A buy signal is generated when the signal line (dark grey line) crosses the MACD (light grey line) from below.

- A sell signal is generated when the signal line (dark grey line) crosses the MACD (light grey line) from above.

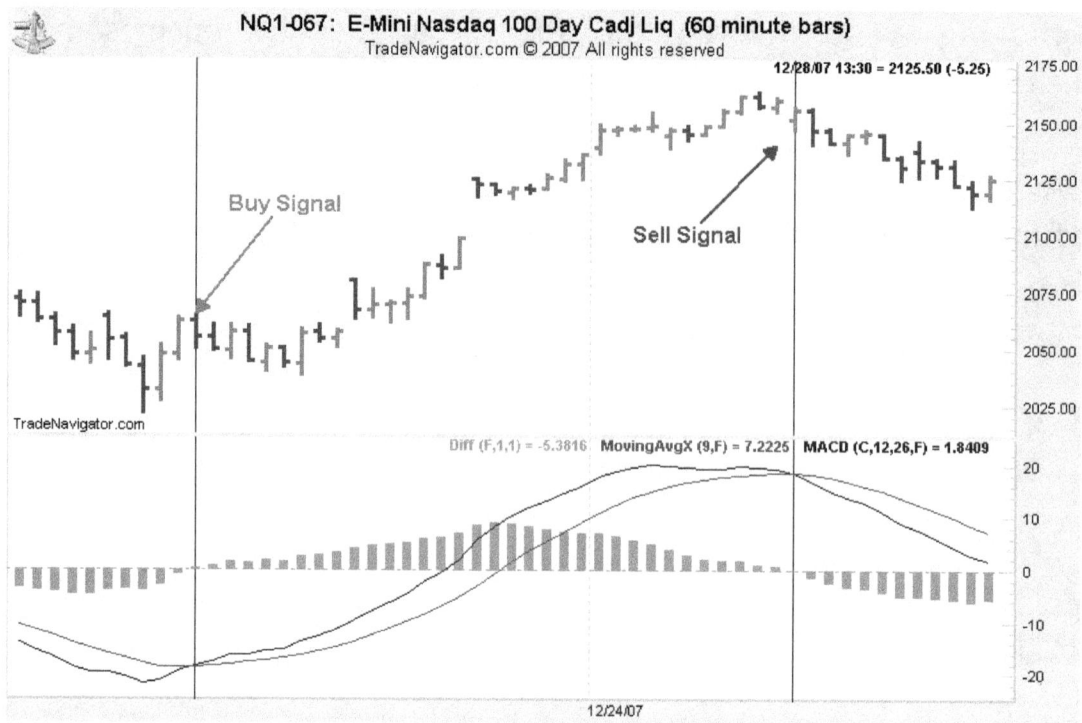

Williams %R

One of the most popular overbought/oversold indicators is Williams %R.

It indicator was developed in 1966 by Larry Williams to help traders identify overbought and oversold positions.

Williams %R, sometimes referred to as %R, compares a stock's close to the high-low range over a specific time.

The formula is quite simple: it subtracts the current day's close from the lowest intraday low of the last 'X' number of days. It then divides Its distance by the highest high minus the lowest previous 'X' number of days. Its computation tells us where, within the next day range, today's close is located. If it's high in the content, it will be in the high percentiles, say over 80%. If we're closing low in the scope of the last 'X' number of days, it would be in the 20% or lower area.

The index has many uses, but the simplest one allows it to identify or suggest an overbought, oversold zone.

The index can be used in all markets and in all timeframes. Most traders use it successfully on intraday bar charts with a parameter of 14 bars.

As stated above, the indicator shows the relationship of the closing price to a high-low range over a specific time, typically 14 bars.

The result is plotted on a chart and oscillates between 0 and 100. The basic idea is that if prices are trading at the high of the high-low range (indicator reading close to 100), then the market is overbought. If the current prices are trading close to the low of the specified range (indicator reading close to 0), then the market is oversold.

- A sell signal is generated when the indicator has a value above 80.

- A buy signal is generated when the indicator has a value below 20.

In It example chart, the %R moves above 80, indicating that Google (GOOG) is "oversold," and a sell signal is generated.

Williams %R works best in sideways-moving markets.

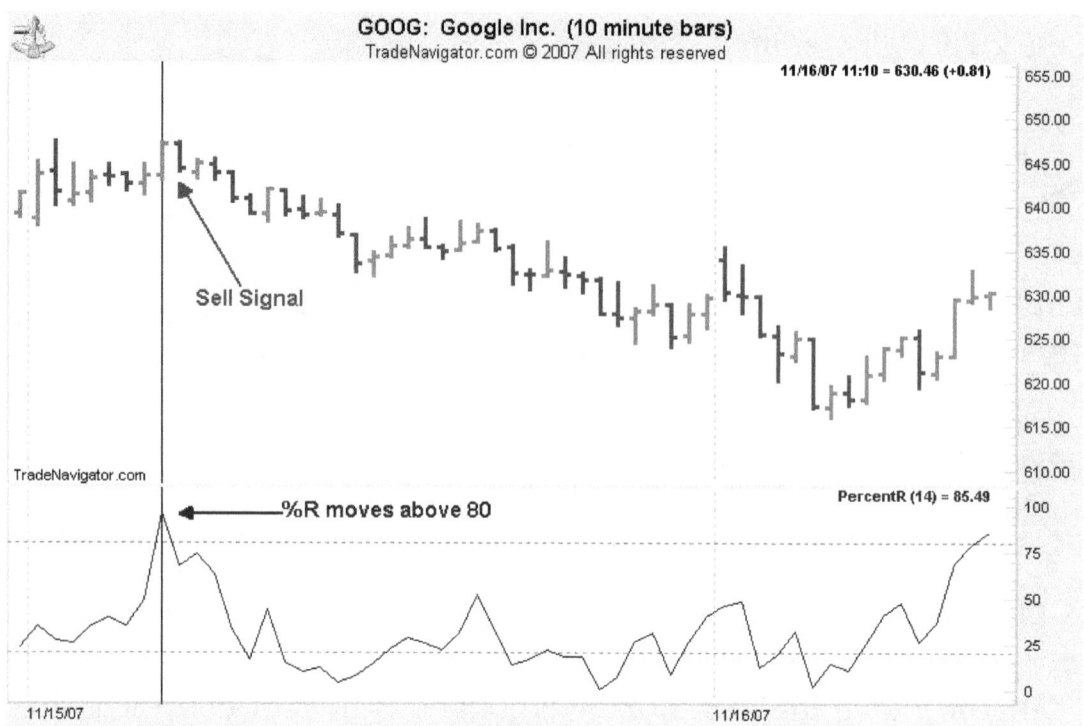

Relative Strength Index (RSI)

Another popular overbought/oversold indicator is the Relative Strength Index (RSI), developed by Welles Wilder. The RSI compares the magnitude of a stock's recent gains to the importance of its recent losses. It turns that information into a number that ranges from 0 to 100. It takes a single parameter – the number of periods – to use in the calculation. In his book, Wilder recommends using 14 periods.

- A sell signal is generated when the RSI crosses the 70-line (overbought-zone) from above.

- A buy signal is generated when the RSI crosses the 30-line (oversold-zone) from below.

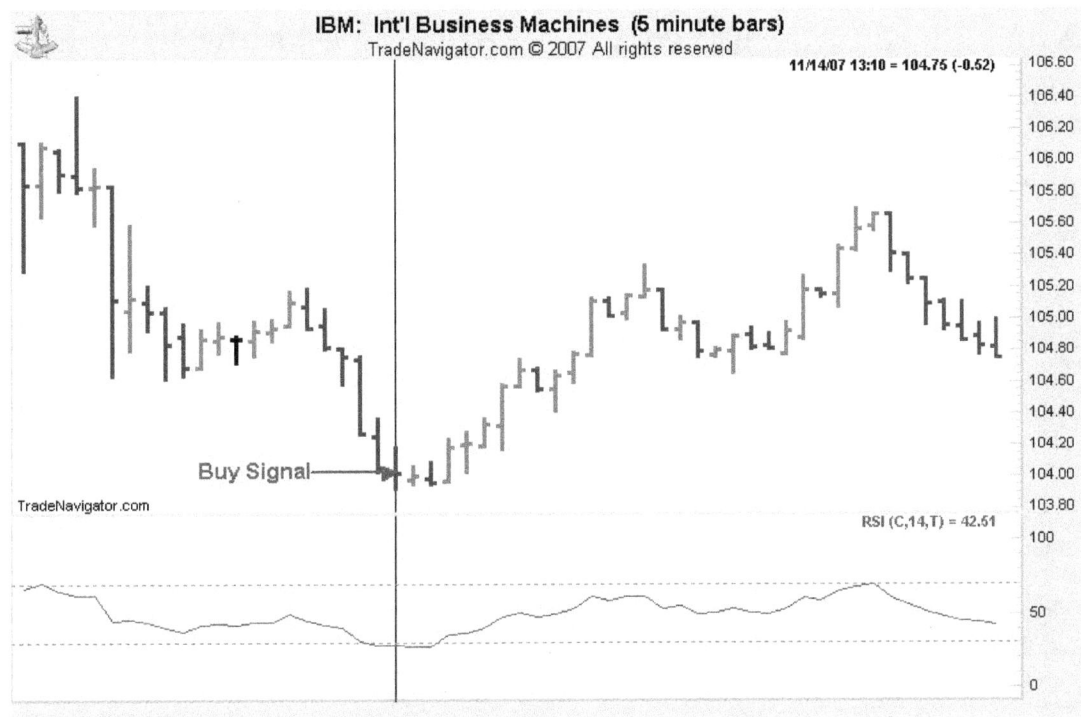

The RSI dips below 30, and a buy signal is generated coincidentally at the day's low. By applying stop loss and profit exit strategies (see next chapter), profits could be realized relatively quickly.

As with the %R, the RSI indicator works best in sideways-moving markets.

Bollinger Bands and Channels

Many traders are familiar with the concept of "Bollinger Bands."

Bollinger Bands consist of a moving average and two standard deviations, one above the moving average and one below. The critical thing to know about Bollinger Bands is that they contain up to 95% of the closing prices, depending on the settings.

The most popular setting is a 21-bar moving average (solid dark grey line) and two standard deviations for the upper and lower band (dotted grey line).

- A buy signal is generated when prices move below the lower Bollinger Band.

- A sell signal is generated when prices move above the upper Bollinger Band.

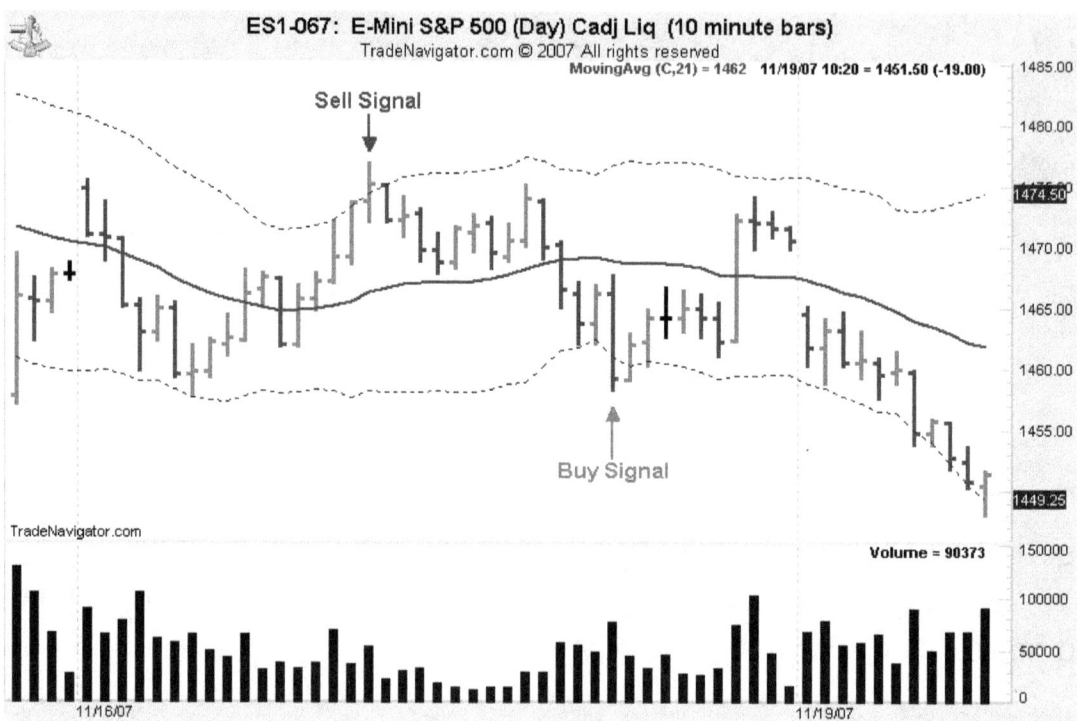

It is a 10-minute chart of the E-mini S&P. After lackluster trading in the morning, prices move above the upper Bollinger Band and generate a sell signal.

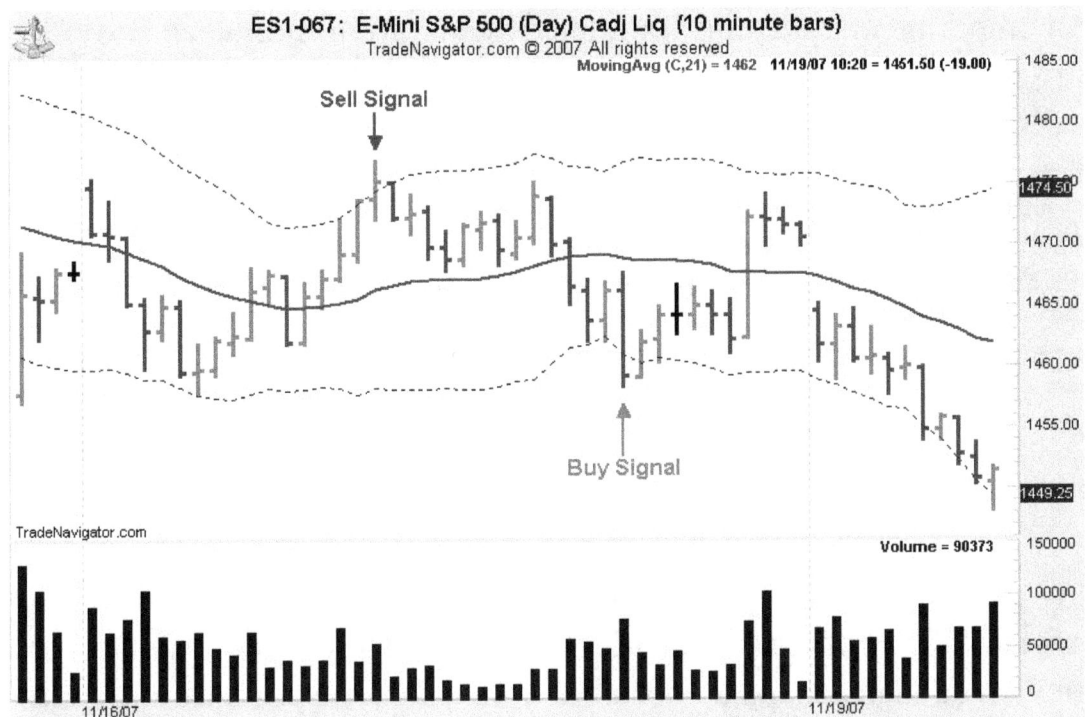

Two hours later, prices move below the lower Bollinger Band and create a buy signal.

It indicator works best in sideways-moving markets.

Trading Approaches

Before deciding on a trading approach, you need to identify whether the market is trending or moving sideways.

Don't fall prey to common mistakes. Many traders simply decide on one trading approach and trade it all the time, whether the market is trending or not. That's a sure way to failure.

Successful traders use multiple trading approaches: they have at least one

> method for a trending market and another system for a sideways moving market. Using the basic principles outlined on page 103, you can determine the market's direction and use the right trading approach.
>
> Don't make the mistake of using only **one** trading approach. Learn to identify whether a market is trending or not and adjust your trading strategy accordingly.

Action Items:

- Pick <u>any</u> chart in <u>any</u> timeframe and practice drawing trendlines. One of the essential skills of a trader is identifying the direction of the market. Practice on as many maps as possible until you can spot a trend within a couple of seconds.

- Select a trading approach that YOU are comfortable with. Ensure that you understand what the indicator you are using is measuring: WHY should you sell when it goes above 80? What EXACTLY does it mean?

- Select a second trading approach. As you know, you should have one for a trending market and one for a market that is going sideways. Which method will you use when?

Crossover of Moving Averages

Another prevalent approach is to use two moving averages: a "fast" moving average (e.g., 14 bars) and a "slow" moving average (e.g., 20 bars). The number of days used for the slow-moving average needs to be larger than the number of days used for the fast-moving average.

- A buy signal is generated when the fast moving average crosses the slow moving average from above.

- A sell signal is generated when the fast moving average crosses the slow moving average from below.

Here's an example of It strategy:

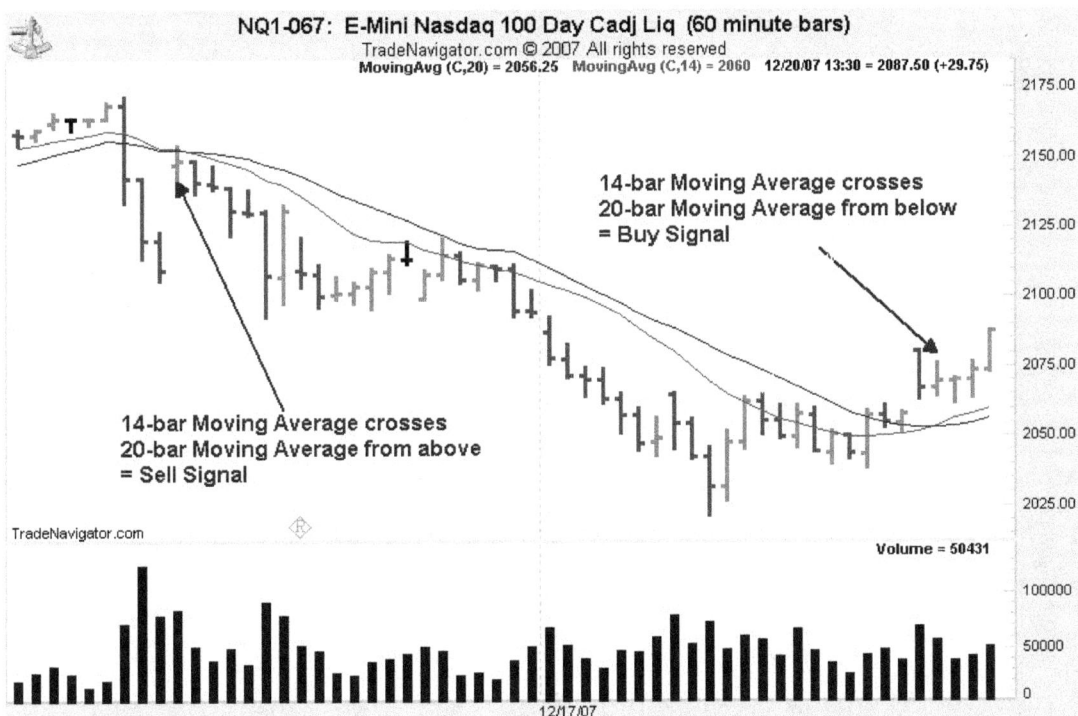

The upper line is the slow-moving average (20 bars), and the lower line is the fast-moving average (14 bars).

Turtle Trading

You'll find plenty of articles on the Internet that will explain the turtle trading rules in detail. The turtles look at the high and the low through the past 20 days and generate the following signals:

- A buy signal is generated when the current prices move higher than the previous 20 bars' high.

- A sell signal is generated when the current prices move lower than the previous 20 bars' low.

Whenever you can draw a resistance line, you can typically draw a corresponding support line, as shown in the following chart.

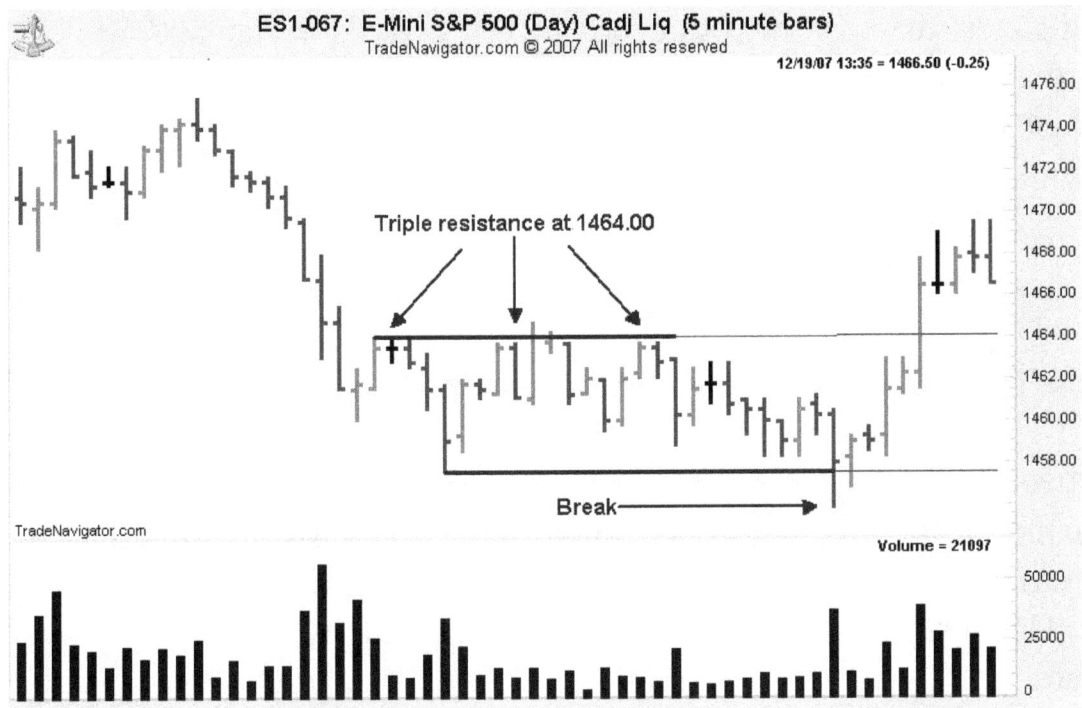

As you can see, the support line holds very well, even though it's broken later. However, the break isn't significant since prices close above the support line.

A Little More on Support and Resistance

Support is the price level at which demand is thought to be strong enough to prevent the price from declining further.

The logic dictates that as the price declines towards support and gets cheaper, buyers become more inclined to buy, and sellers become less willing to sell. By the time the price reaches the support level, it's believed that demand will overcome supply and prevent the price from falling below support.

Resistance is the price level at which selling is thought to be strong enough to prevent the price from rising further.

The logic dictates that as the price advances towards resistance, sellers become more inclined to sell, and buyers become less willing to buy. By the time the price reaches the resistance level, it's believed that supply will overcome demand and prevent the price from rising above resistance.

Trendlines & Trend Channels

Trendlines are helpful yet straightforward tools in confirming the direction of market trends. An upward straight line is drawn by connecting at least two successive lows. Naturally, the second point must be higher than the first.
The continuation of the line helps determine the path along which the market will move. An upward trend is a concrete method to identify support lines/levels. Conversely, downward lines are charted by connecting two points or more. The validity of a trading line is partly related to the number of connection points. Yet it's worth mentioning that points must not be too close together.

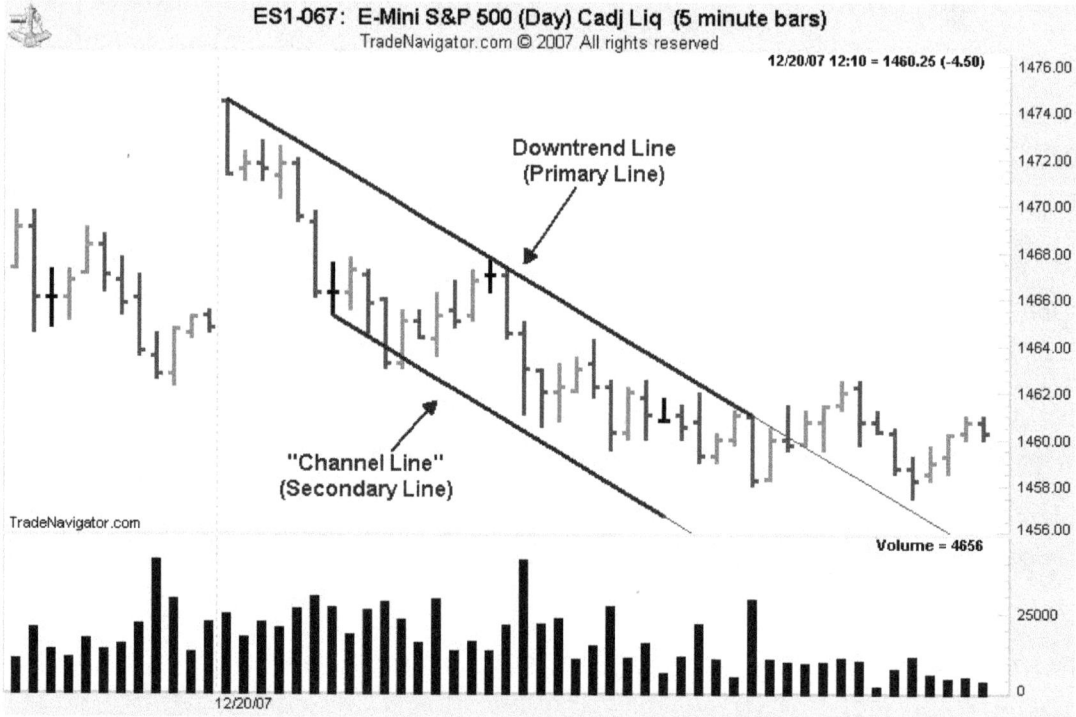

A channel is defined as the price path drawn by two parallel trendlines. The lines serve as an upward, the downward, or straight corridor for the price.

When drawing trend channels, you first remove the trendline and then construct the "channel line" as a parallel line to the primary trendline.

Trend channels are typically constructed to derive entry and exit points in an uptrend or downtrend.

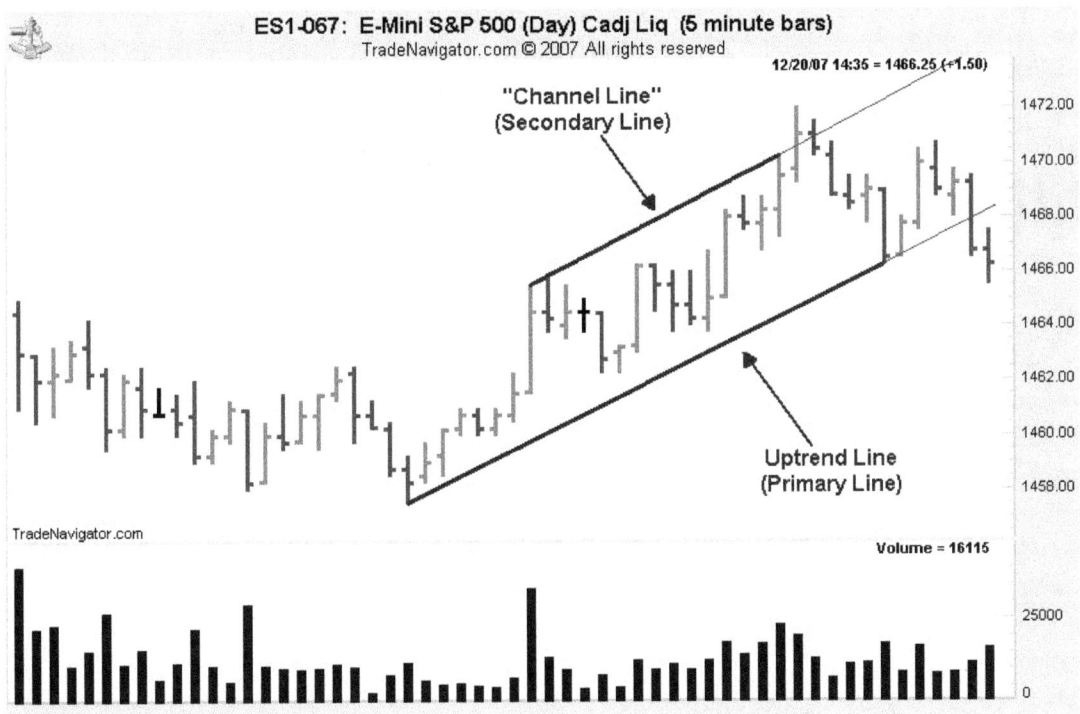

In a downtrend, you'd sell at the primary downtrend line and buy back at the secondary channel line, as shown in the following example:

Popular Trading Approaches

By now, you know that any market is either trending or moving sideways. Therefore you'll apply one of the following two trading strategies:

1.) **Trend-following** – when prices are moving up, you buy, and when prices are going down, you sell.

2.) **Trend-fading** – when prices are trading at an extreme (e.g., the upper band of a channel), you sell, and then you try to catch the small move while prices are shifting back into "normalcy." The same applies to buying.

Most indicators that you'll find in your charting software belong to one of these two categories: indicators for identifying trends (e.g., moving averages) or hands that define overbought or oversold situations, which offer you a trade setup for a short-term swing trade.

Don't become confused by all the possibilities of entering a trade. Just make sure that you understand WHY you're using a specific indicator and WHAT that indicator is measuring.

Here are some examples of popular trading approaches:

Trend-following:

1.) Moving Averages
2.) Crossover of Moving Averages
3.) Turtle Trading
4.) Moving Average Convergence-Divergence (MACD)

Trend-fading:

1.) Williams %R

2.) Relative Strength Index (RSI)
3.) Bollinger Bands and Channels

Simple Moving Averages

If you believe in the "trend-is-your-friend" tenet of technical analysis, moving averages (M.A.) are very helpful. Moving averages tell the average price in a given point of time over a defined time, typically the closing price. They're called 'moving' because they reflect the latest average while adhering to the same time.

A weakness of moving averages is that they lag the market, so they do not necessarily signal a change in trends. To address It issue, use a shorter period, such as a 5- or 10-day moving average, more reflective of the recent price action than the 40- or 200-day moving averages. The concept is simple:

- A buy signal is generated when the closing price moves above the moving average.

- A sell signal is generated when the closing price dips below the moving average.

Here's an example using the 10-minute chart of Amazon (AMZN):

You can see that Its strategy works very well in trending markets (see first buy signal). Still, in sideways moving needs, you're getting whipsawed (see second buy signal).

The Right Concept for the Right Market
Every day, a lot of traders attempt to use strategies based on moving averages. And then they complain that these strategies don't work. Keep in mind that It is a trend-following strategy – you should only apply it in trending markets. You might want to use trendlines or other indicators to ensure that the market you're watching is trending, and then use moving averages to get your specific entry signals.

****

Chapter 10

How to Develop Your Own Profitable Day Trading Strategy

Developing a profitable trading strategy is not as complicated as you might be led to believe. Many people will tell you that it's challenging to build your trading system, but it's pretty straightforward. The next part of It book will show you how to develop your trading strategy in seven simple but essential steps.

    Step 1: Selecting a Market

    Step 2: Selecting a Timeframe

    Step 3: Selecting a Trading Style

    Step 4: Defining Entry Points

    Step 5: Defining Exit Points

    Step 6: Evaluating Your Trading Strategy

Step 7: Improving Your Trading Strategy

Step 1: Selecting a Market

With the fame of online trading, more and more financial instruments are available to trade. You have a variety of choices, not just stocks, options, and futures. In recent years, financial instruments like Exchange Traded Funds (ETFs), Single Stock Futures (SSF), and the Foreign Exchange Market (forex) have become available for the private investor.

Besides, the existing financial instruments have been enhanced. Exchanges started introducing electronic contracts and mini contracts of popular commodities like gold, silver, crude oil, natural gas, and grains. These futures contracts have become very popular amongst day traders. The volume of the mini and electronic contracts quickly surpassed the work of the pit-traded commodities.

These days, you can trade ANYTHING. For example, suppose you want to participate in the real estate market without owning properties. In that case, you can invest in Real Estate Investment Trusts (REITs), or even Real Estate Futures of a particular area, like Chicago or Denver (traded at the CME).

This chapter will focus on the four main markets: stocks, forex, futures, and stock options. We'll examine each of these markets according to the following criteria:

1.) Low Initial Capital Requirements

Low initial capital means that you can start your day trading activities with a low initial deposit. It's always better to trade with small money and then move up to more considerable capital when you're comfortable enough with the market.

2.) Leverage

Leverage is the second key. With sound risk management in place, highly leveraged markets allow us to place a small amount of capital into the market and realize more enormous profit potentials. It will enable us to build up a short account quickly.

3.) Liquidity

The third factor is liquidity. We'll focus on liquid markets to avoid problems caused by market manipulation and slippage. When trading a call, we want to ensure that we receive quick and accurate fills for our orders. A large order placed by a market-maker or broker does not erratically move the market.

4.) Volatility

The fourth factor is volatility. You can make money in any market, as long as it's moving. A market that's just going sideways and doesn't move in any direction is tough to trade. It's easier to change a call that's either going up or going down.

Throughout It book, you'll learn how to trade <u>any</u> market, but it certainly helps to know something about the market you're selling. So, we'll include a brief description of needs and participants at the beginning of each of the following sections.

Trading Stocks

The stock market is a private or public market for trading company stock at an agreed price. Investors give companies value. The value of the company is divided into many shares. These shares can be bought or sold (raising or lowering the value of the company).

When you buy stocks, you essentially own a little piece of that company whose shares you just bought. You'll become a shareholder. So, the more shares you buy, the larger the portion of the company you own. If the value of the company rises, the value of your shares rises. If the value of the company decreases, the value of your shares decreases.

When the company makes a profit, you may receive some of that profit in dividends; the profit is shared amongst all the people who own the stock.

Ownership of shares usually is called equity.

There are two main types of stocks – **preferred stock** and **common stock** – and there are many advantages to owning preferred stock over common stock. Here are the main ones:

1. When you're holding preferred stock, the dividend is paid to you <u>before</u> any dividends are paid to common stockholders.

2. Preferred stock typically pays a <u>fixed</u> dividend that does not fluctuate, unlike the common stock's dividend.

3. Owners of preferred stocks have a more extraordinary claim on the company's assets. For example, in case of bankruptcy, preferred stockholders are paid <u>first</u>, before common stockholders.

However, as a day trader, you don't have to worry about the different kinds of stocks or dividend yields since you're just holding a store for a few minutes or hours.

Avoiding Stock Trading Scams

If you have an email account, you've probably received many emails with

Free Stock Trading Tips. In these emails, somebody recommends a "hot stock."

If you were to follow these tips, you'd probably end up getting caught in a so-called "pump-and-dump" scheme.

Here's how it works:
These so-called stock picking services buy a particular stock that's usually trading at $0.02-$0.30. These stocks are often not listed on the exchanges, and the volume is typically only a few thousand shares per day.

After these stock picking services buy tens of thousands of these shares, they recommend their subscribers. You'll find that it's not easy to buy these stocks since they're not listed on regular stock exchanges. And, if you ask your broker to buy It stock for you, you might end up paying 4-5 times more than usual in commissions.

The stock picking service is now hoping that many of their subscribers will start buying It stock. They typically say, "It's trading now at $0.02, and it should go up to $0.12." That would be a whopping 600% increase! Since stock traders are greedy by nature, many will probably start buying It stock. Since there is a sudden demand, the stock prices will go up – initially.

But, before the stock hits the predicted exit price, the stock-picking service starts selling (or dumping) the shares that they bought BEFORE they recommended it to you.

Since they bought such a large amount of It stock, there's suddenly an enormous supply available again, and prices start falling. More and more investors panic and sell their stores, which drives the stock prices even further down.

After a massive sell-off, the stock is generally trading at the same level. It was BEFORE the stock-picking service started recommending it. And, in some cases, it'll be much lower, resulting in a loss for whoever was drawn into the trap. So, investors are losing their money, and the only winner is the stock-picking service.

Here's an example of a "pump-and-dump" scheme:

The following image is a screenshot from an online service that is offering "Free Stock Tips."

Let's check the stock market against our criteria:

    1.) **Capital Requirements**

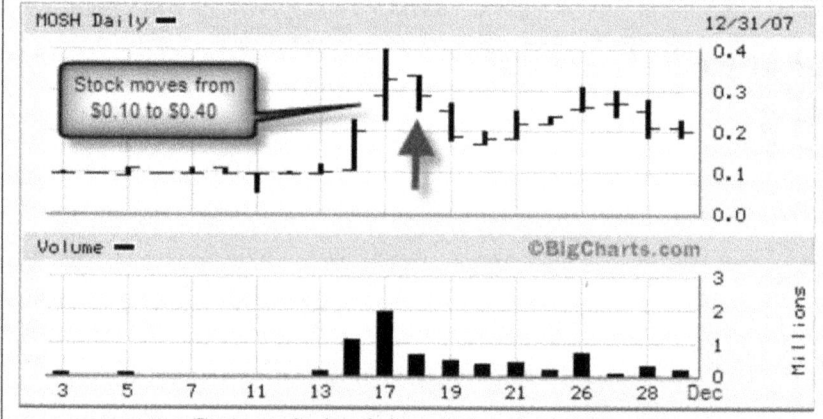

In August and September of 2001, the NYSE and NASD established the Pattern Day Trading Rule. Its rules dictate that "if a trader executes four or more day trades within a five-business-day period, then he must maintain a minimum equity of $25,000 in his margin account at all times." It means that you need at least $28,000-$30,000 if you want to day trade stocks because you need a "cushion" if you experience losses.

2.) Leverage

When trading stocks, you can either open a "cash account" or a "margin account." When you open a cash account, you can buy or sell the stock for precisely the amount you have in your account – i.e., your leverage is 1:1.

When you open a margin account, you can trade stocks on margin. Buying on margin is borrowing money from a broker to purchase stock. You can think of it as a loan from your brokerage. Margin trading allows you to buy more stock than you'd be able to normally. An initial investment of at least $2,000 is required for a margin account, though some brokerages require more. Its deposit is known as the minimum margin. Once the account is opened and operational, you can borrow up to 50% of a stock's purchase price.

Example: Let's say that you deposit $10,000 in your margin account. Because you put up 50% of the purchase price, It means you have $20,000 worth of buying power. Then, if you buy the $5,000 value of the stock, you still have $15,000 in buying power remaining. In Its case, your leverage is 1:2.

Suppose you have developed a good relationship with your broker. In that case, he might even allow you to borrow up to 80% of your initial deposit, giving you a leverage of 1:8.

3.) Liquidity

Currently, there are more than 10,000 stocks available on U.S. stock exchanges. Around 900 stores have an average daily volume of more than 2,000,000 shares traded, and more than 600 of them are traded with over 3,000,000 shares per day. If you focus on these stocks, you won't have a problem with market manipulation or slippage.

4.) **Volatility**

In 2007, the average daily movement of the stocks in the Dow Jones Index was between 1% and 2%, and many of these stocks moved even more dramatically than that:

- Alcoa, Inc. (A.A.) moved between 2% and 5% per day

- American Intl. Group (AIG) moved between 2% and 8% per day

- American Express (AXP) moved between 2% and 6% per day

And that's just naming the first three stocks of the Dow Jones. Volatility has NOT been a problem in the stock markets, especially in 2007.

Conclusion:

Stock markets have adequate liquidity and volatility, but the initial capital requirements are high ($25,000), and the maximum leverage is only 1:8.

Trading Forex

Its market may sound complicated and frightening to tackle, but trust me, it's not. Like any other type of trading, the basic rule in the forex market is that you have to buy when the market is going up and sell when the market is going down.

The word "forex" comes from **For**eign **Ex**change, and forex is often abbreviated to F.X.

Forex trading involves the buying and selling of currencies. In simpler terms, it's the exchange of one money for another at an agreed-upon rate.

If you've ever traveled to another country, chances are you've traded your currency against the local country's currency. If you've done It, you have a good idea of how forex trading works.

All the currency of the world is involved in the forex market. It may be confusing to choose which one to trade, but all you need to know are the major currencies, which are the most frequently traded.

Here are the major currencies:

1.) U.S. Dollar (USD)
2.) Japanese Yen (JPY)
3.) British Pound (GBP)
4.) Swiss Franc (CHF)
5.) European Union Euro (EUR)
6.) Australian Dollar (AUD)
7.) New Zealand Dollar (NZD)
8.) Canadian Dollar (CAD)

The next thing you need to know is that forex is traded in currency pairs. Trading currency pairs means you're buying one currency while simultaneously selling another currency.

Examples:

The most heavily traded products in the forex market are typical:

- EUR/USD
- USD/JPY
- GBP/USD

You need to know that the forex markets are extremely volatile. You can easily make (or lose) thousands of dollars in a single day.

Many forex brokers offer "free quotes and charts" and "no commissions," but keep in mind that nothing is for free. You are paying a spread – i.e., you CANNOT buy a currency and immediately sell it for the same amount.

It's like at the exchange booths when you're on vacation: you might exchange $100 into 80 Euro, but when you change the 80 Euro back into dollars, you only receive $96. The same concept applies when trading forex: you're paying at least 2 "pips." It amounts to approximately $20, depending on the currency pair you're trading.

The forex markets can be tricky – they shouldn't be taken lightly.

Another disadvantage of forex trading is that you're NOT trading at an exchange: **there is no "Foreign Exchange."**

You're trading against your broker: if you're selling, then your broker is buying from you, and vice versa. And that's why your broker is giving you the quotes for free: he can give you *any* quote he chooses since there are no regulations.

Example:

Take a look at these forex quotes. All three of the following screenshots were taken on Tuesday, January 1, 2007, at 3:00 pm U.S. Eastern Time.

Note: The time in the first two charts is displayed at GMT (+6 hours). I used three different websites to obtain these quotes:

Symbol*	Bid	Ask	High	Low	Open	Change	Time	Favs
XAUUSD	↓833.4	↓833.9	838.9	833.67	833.84	↑0.1	02:13	Add
XAGUSD	•14.78	•14.83	14.84	14.8125	14.83	•0	14:00	Add
EURGBP	↑0.7344	↑0.7348	0.7364	0.7342	0.73477	•0	15:01	Add
EURUSD	↓1.4586	↓1.4598	1.464	1.458	1.4598	↓-0.0005	15:01	Add
EURJPY	↑162.79	↑162.82	163.42	162.5	162.747	↑0.07	15:00	Add
EURZAR	↑9.9586	↑9.9886	10.0263	9.9625	10.0031	↓-0.0145	15:00	Add
EURCHF	↓1.654	↓1.6543	1.6576	1.6393	1.6541	↑0.0002	15:00	Add
EURCAD	↑1.4494	↑1.4502	1.4601	1.4488	1.4511	↓-0.0009	14:59	Add
EURAUD	↓1.6657	↓1.6667	1.6743	1.6651	1.6662	↑0.0005	15:00	Add
EURNZD	↑1.9033	↑1.9053	1.9118	1.9029	1.90544	↓-0.0001	15:00	Add
EURSEK	↑9.4423	↑9.4463	9.4511	9.4242	9.4401	↑0.0062	15:01	Add
EURSGD	↓2.0749	↓2.1249	2.1295	2.1004	2.1046	↑0.0203	15:01	Add

Name	Bid	Ask	Change	%Change	High	Low	Time
EUR/USD	1.4586	1.4589	0.0001	0.01 %	**1.4611**	1.4577	19:59
GBP/USD	1.9861 ↓	1.9866 ↓	0.00 ↓	0.00 % ↓	1.987	1.9838	20:00
USD/JPY	111.54	111.58	-0.12	-0.11 %	111.76	111.30	19:56
USD/CHF	1.1341	1.1351	0.0016	0.14 %	1.1347	1.1313	19:58
USD/NOK	5.4372 ↑	5.4462 ↑	0.0024 ↑	0.04 %	5.4474	5.4279	20:00
USD/DKK	5.1088 ↑	5.1138 ↑	-0.002 ↑	-0.04 %	5.1141	5.0989	20:00
USD/SEK	6.4687 ↑	6.4767 ↑	0.0088 ↑	0.14 % ↑	6.4747	6.43	20:00
USD/CAD	0.9936 ↓	0.994 ↓	-0.0042 ↓	-0.42 % ↓	0.9978	0.993	20:00
NZD/USD	0.7663	0.7671	0.0007	0.09 %	0.7663	0.7637	19:03
AUD/USD	0.8755	0.8758	0.0002	0.02 %	0.8769	0.8744	19:59
USD/MXN	10.911	10.941	-0.0046	-0.04 %	10.9156	10.894	19:02
USD/SGD	1.4395	1.44	-0.0014	-0.10 %	1.4409	1.4381	20:00

Solution by NetDania   Data Source: Comstock llc

Take a look at It day's high of the USD/EUR currency pair:

1.) The first data source reports it at **1.4611**.
2.) The second data source shows **1.4748**. 3.) The third data source reports a high of **1.4640**.

Major Currencies - Real-Time

Currency	Bid	Ask	Change	High	Low	Time
EUR/USD				**1.4748**	1.4567	20:01.00
USD/JPY				112.29	111.2	20:02.00
GBP/USD	1.9855	1.9874		2.0101	1.9788	17:59.00
USD/CHF			0.0013 ↑	1.1372	1.1199	20:01.00
USD/CAD	0.9936 ↑	0.994		0.9986	0.9763	19:58.00
AUD/USD	0.8757 ↑		0.0009 ↑	0.8827	0.8733	20:02.00
EUR/JPY				165.5	162.3	20:01.00
EUR/CHF			0.00	1.6587	1.6381	20:02.00
GBP/JPY	221.52 ↑	221.59 ↑		224.91	220.84	20:02.00
GBP/CHF			0.0033 ↑	2.2625	2.2241	19:59.00
CHF/JPY				99.86	98.14	20:02.00
NZD/USD	0.7661 ↑	0.7666 ↑	0.0009 ↑	0.7794	0.7645	20:00.00
USD/ZAR	6.825	6.845	0.0255 ↑	6.8665	6.762	19:00.00
Gold	833.4	833.9		843.8	829.4	07:13.00
Silver	14.78	14.83	0.00	14.92	14.66	19:00.00

That's a difference of 137 ticks, which equals $1,370! Do you see the problem? Forex prices are entirely subjective.

Let's check forex trading against our criteria:

1.) **Capital Requirements**

   Many forex brokers let you start with as little as $1,000 in your trading account.

2.) **Leverage**

   The typical leverage in the forex market is 1:100 – i.e., for every $1,000 in your trading account, you can trade $100,000. Recently, forex brokers started offering leverage of 1:200, allowing you to sell $100,000 for every $500 in your trading account.

Mini-Forex Trading

Although the capital requirements for trading the forex markets are already low, "Mini-Forex Trading" has become very popular recently. Mini-forex trading is good for people who have just started in the forex market and who don't have enough funds to open a regular account. It requires a smaller amount of capital compared to regular forex accounts – a minimum of $250. On It account, you can trade up to 5 mini lots. A mini lot is only 1/10th the size of a standard forex account.

Example:

On a regular account, a 25-pip stop loss is equal to a loss of $250. Since a mini-forex account is just 1/10th of the standard forex account, It stop loss amounts to only $25. Instead of trading in 100,000 units, you are trading in 10,000 units.

What are the perks of mini-forex trading?

Even with just a small stake involved, you still get to enjoy benefits such as a free trading platform – just like regular forex traders. A few other benefits include state-of-the art trading software, charts, and resources. In It way, you can build up your confidence in your trading skills while slowly increasing your profits and trading position in the market. You get to manage your money on a small scale before going for the higher stakes in regular forex trading.

You can also develop a sound trading strategy without getting too emotionally involved in possible profits or losses. For practice, newbies can start with paper trading; in the real market, they can start small with mini-forex trading.

Conclusion:

Mini-forex trading requires a smaller amount of capital and less emotional investment, and it provides the perfect opportunity for you to slowly build up your skills and confidence as a trader. In a way, it prepares you for the higher stakes of the more advanced world of foreign exchange trading.

3.) Liquidity

It is certainly not a problem in the forex market. Unfortunately, since the forex market is decentralized and there's no official exchange, you can't get real-time volume data.

But, according to the Triennial Central Bank Survey of 2007, the average turnover in the traditional foreign exchange market is around $3.21 trillion daily, and it's still growing.

Here are the daily averages of turnover on the forex market over the last 15 years:

$880 billion (April of 1992)
$1.15 trillion (April of 1995)
$1.65 trillion (April of 1998)
$1.42 trillion (April of 2001)
$1.97 trillion (April of 2004)
$3.21 trillion (April of 2007)

Source: Triennial Central Bank Survey – December 2007, www.bis.org

4.) Volatility

You will find decent volatility in the forex market. It's not as great as in the stock market. Still, because of the too high leverage, even small movements can yield substantial profits. Here are the average daily activities for three different currency pairs:

EUR/USD -   between 0.5% and 1% per day
USD/JPY -   between 0.5% and 1.5% per day
GBP/USD -   between 0.5% and 1.5% per day

Keep in mind that these moves represent approximately $750 - $1,500 per day for each $100,000 traded.

Conclusion:

Forex markets are too liquid, and the capital requirements are as low as $1,000. The leverage is at least 100:1, and there's decent volatility. Overall, forex seems to be an excellent market to trade, but keep in mind that there are some disadvantages, too, as mentioned earlier in the It section.

Trading Futures
Futures trading continues to grow in popularity, and many traders are jumping into It type of investing.

Futures trading offers many advantages, especially if you're new to trading. Yet, many traders shy away from futures trading because they're not familiar with it.

There's a lot of misunderstanding when it comes to the future. People often think that futures are precarious and challenging to trade. To some extent, that's true. Thanks to high leverage, futures trading I.S. riskier than stock trading.

However, futures trading – BECAUSE of the high leverage – also provides an excellent opportunity for the private trader.

So what are futures? Futures contracts simply called lots, are exchange-traded derivatives. They are standardized contracts among buyers and sellers of commodities that specify the amount of an entity, the grade/quality, and the delivery location. These futures contracts are typically traded at futures exchanges, like the Chicago Board of Trade (CBOT), the Chicago Mercantile Exchange (CME), the New York Mercantile Exchange (NYMEX), and others.

Below is a list of different types of futures contracts:

1.) **Currencies** – The currency market is probably the best-known commodity available, dealing in the British Pound, the American Dollar, the European Euro, etc.

2.) **Interest Rates** – Interest rates are traded in two ways on It market: T-Bonds represent long-term interest rates. At the same time, T-Bills are used for short-term interest rates.

3.) **Energies** – A variety of fuel commodities are traded on It market, including natural gas, heating oil, and crude oil futures.

4.) **Food Sector** – Sugar, coffee, and orange juice are just a few of the regular goods traded in It sector.

5.) **Metals** – Commodities in It market are relatively well-known, such as copper, gold, and silver.

6.) **Agricultural** – Futures in It market include wheat, corn, coffee, and soybeans.

Futures are not borrowed like stock. Therefore, initiating a short position is just as expected and easy as buying the lots.

> A Little Bit of History
>
> Trading on commodities began in early 18th century Japan, with rice and silk trading, and similarly in Holland, with tulip bulbs. Trading in the U.S. began in the mid-19th century when central grain markets were established. A marketplace was created for farmers to bring their commodities and sell them either for immediate delivery (called the spot or cash market) or forwarding delivery. All contract trading began with traditional items such as grains, meat, and livestock.
>
> These days, exchange trading has expanded to include metals, energy, currencies, currency indices, equities, equity indices, government interest rates, and private interest rates. Contracts on the financial instruments were introduced in the 1970s by the Chicago Mercantile Exchange. These instruments became hugely successful and quickly overtook commodities futures in terms of trading volume and global accessibility.

The Commodities Future Trading Commissions (CFTC), an independent agency of the United States government, regulates all futures transactions in the United States. Several factors, including the nature of the underlying asset, when it must be delivered, the currency of the transaction, and at what date the contract stops trading, as well as the tick size or minimum legal change in price, characterizes each futures contract.

Here's a list of the five most popular futures contracts:

>   1.) **S&P 500 E-mini** – It contract has all of the advantages of the S&P 500, but the investment cost is much lower. It can be traded electronically five days a week, almost 24 hours a

day. It's become prevalent in the futures markets.

2.) **E-mini NASDAQ 100** – As with the S&P 500, Its contract is electronically traded; it tracks the NASDAQ 100. The margin amount required to change is significantly smaller than a standard warranty. Since not all traders have the funds to trade on the regular NASDAQ 100, It E-mini is the perfect solution.

3.) **Light Sweet Crude Oil** – Oil futures are one of the most well-known commodities out there. Every time you hear about "the price of oil" in the paper or on the news, It is the contract they're talking about.

4.) **Gold** – The gold futures contract is also popular. In the 1970s, the United States adopted the Gold Standard, creating an essential place in the U.S. economy for gold. Since that time, the gold price has gone through regular, dramatic changes. Those changes are usually in the opposite direction of the U.S. dollar. The gold futures contract follows the differences in price per ounce of gold, and gold investments are frequently used in hedge funds.

5.) **E-mini Euro F.X.** – The E-mini Euro F.X. contract moves with the exchange rate between the European Euro and the U.S. dollar. As with the rest of the E-mini deals, the margin amounts required to trade the Euro F.X. are much lower than the standard contract amounts, which means that It contract presents a fantastic opportunity for traders who don't have accounts large enough to trade the legal arrangements.

The growing popularity of futures trading stems from the fact that only a relatively small amount of money, known as initial margin, is required to buy or sell a futures contract. By definition, these futures margins are a good faith deposit to ensure that the market participants are legitimate.

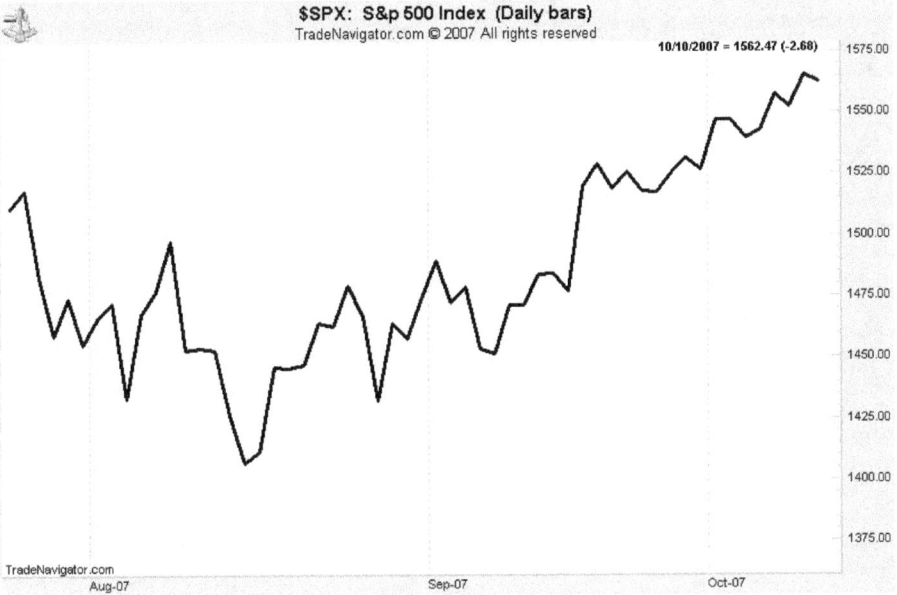

Whenever you open a position by buying or selling futures, you will pay a small initial margin.

The advantage is that the initial margin on a stock future is much less than the cost of buying the actual stock outright.

Example:

The following graphic shows an actual stock index, the S&P 500.
Its index <u>could</u> rise from 1560 to 1570. As of October 12, 2007, it is trading at around 1561.80. Some people think it's less risky to switch the whole market index rather than an individual stock. Therefore, the stock exchanges have introduced an artificial inventory named the SPY (also called the SPYDER contract).

The SPY stock mirrors the S&P 500 Index because you cannot trade the whole index traditionally. If you wanted to change the entire S&P 500 index, you would have to buy all 500 stocks in the index. You can't do It. To make it affordable for private traders, the SPY is divided by ten.

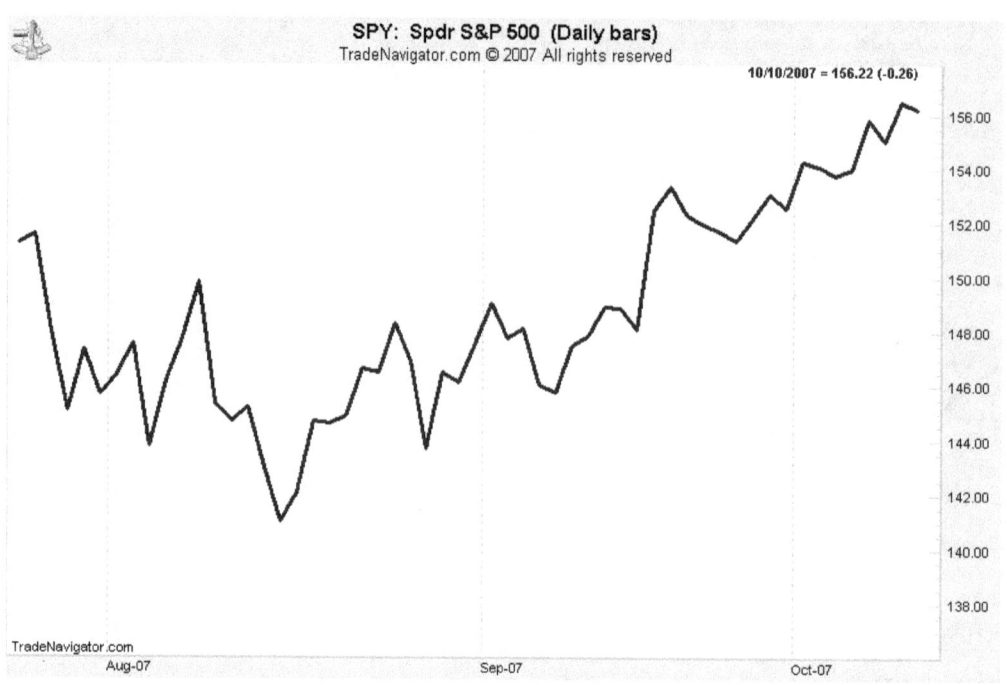

So, we're tracking the index, and the synthetic stock is reduced by a factor of 10 – it's trading at 156. If the SPX (the index) moves from 1560 to 1570, the SPY will move from 156 to 157.

If you're trading one share of SPY, you will make or lose one dollar. And how much capital is needed to trade one share? 156 dollars.

So, for 156 dollars, you will be rewarded with a one-dollar profit if the whole index moves by 10 points.

If you were trading 500 shares of the SPY, you would make 500 dollars on a move of 10 points. The capital needed for 500 shares is much higher than for one share. The required money is 156 dollars per share, times the 500 shares you would want to trade.

The total amount of capital needed to trade 500 shares would be 78,000 dollars.

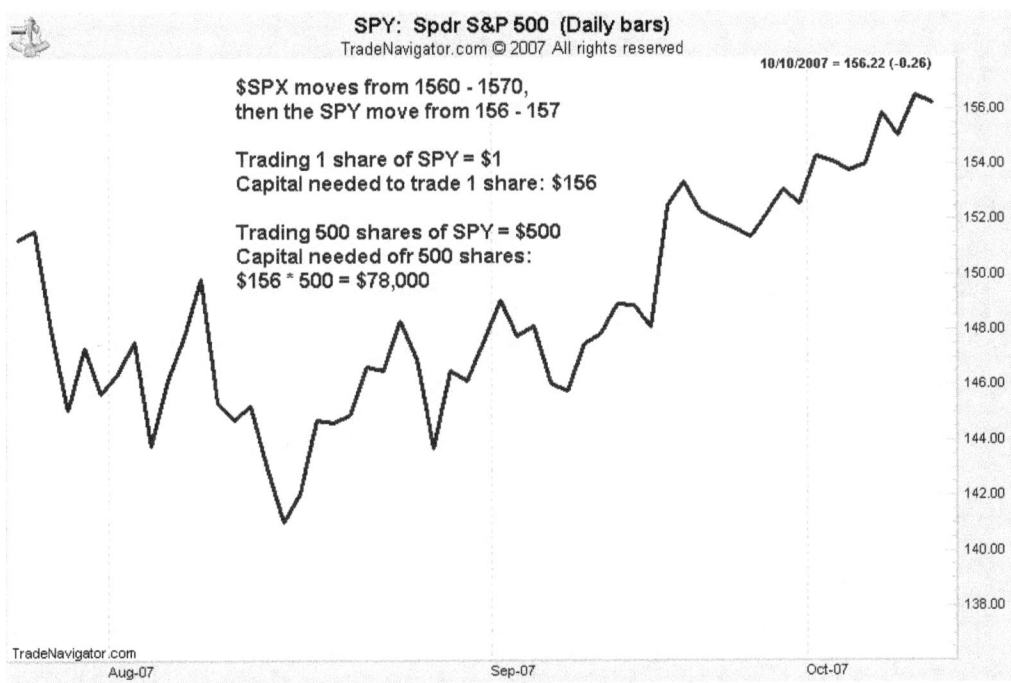

Seventy-eight thousand dollars is quite a lot. The thing to look at here is your return on investment, which most traders use to measure their success.

If you make five hundred dollars after investing 78,000 dollars, the return on that investment would be 0.6%. That's a minimal amount for a 10-point move in the underlying index.

It is precisely why we have the futures markets. There's enormous leverage in the futures markets because you only have to deposit a relatively small amount of money (initial margin). Now, the following chart shows the futures contracts, the so-called Emini S&P:

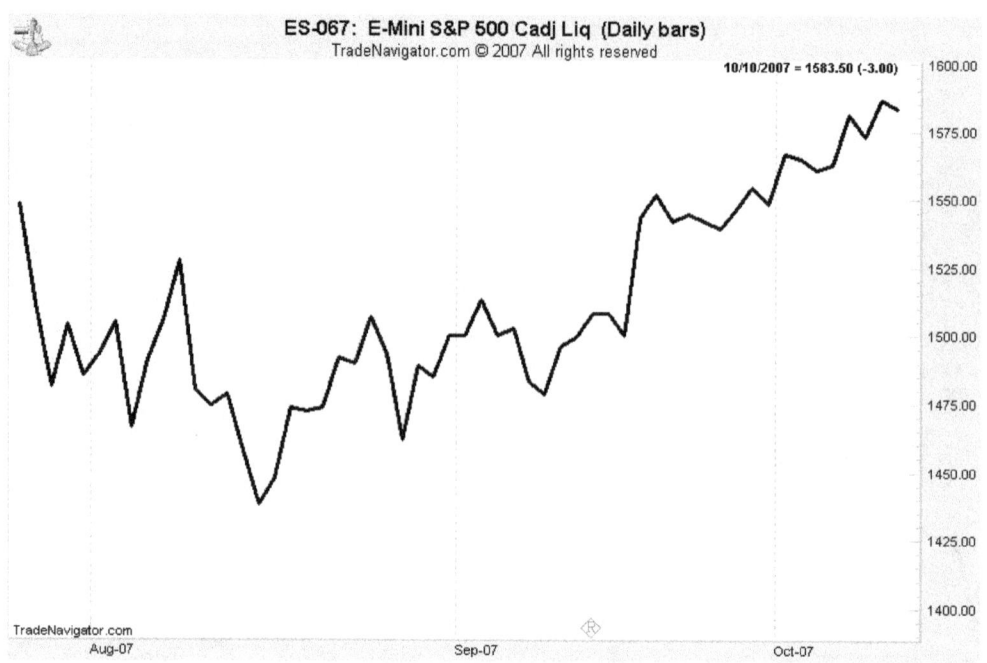

You'll see that the E-mini is tracking the index much closer – here, we're looking at a current value of 1574.50. The critical thing to know is that if the E-mini S&P – which is also abbreviated as E.S. – moves from 1560 to 1570, you would make 500 dollars per contract.

And how much of an investment is required to make 500 dollars off one contract in It move?

About 4,000 dollars. The margin requirement for the E-mini S&P is approximately 4,000 dollars. And if you're day trading it, you even get a discount, which means you'll only have to pay 2,000 dollars. Sometimes, it's even as little as $1,000.

So, you can deposit 4,000 dollars and participate in a 10-point move for a profit of 500 dollars. Let's calculate our return on that initial investment.

Instead of 0.6%, we are looking at 12.5%. That's more than twenty times the return you would have gotten using the SPY contract.

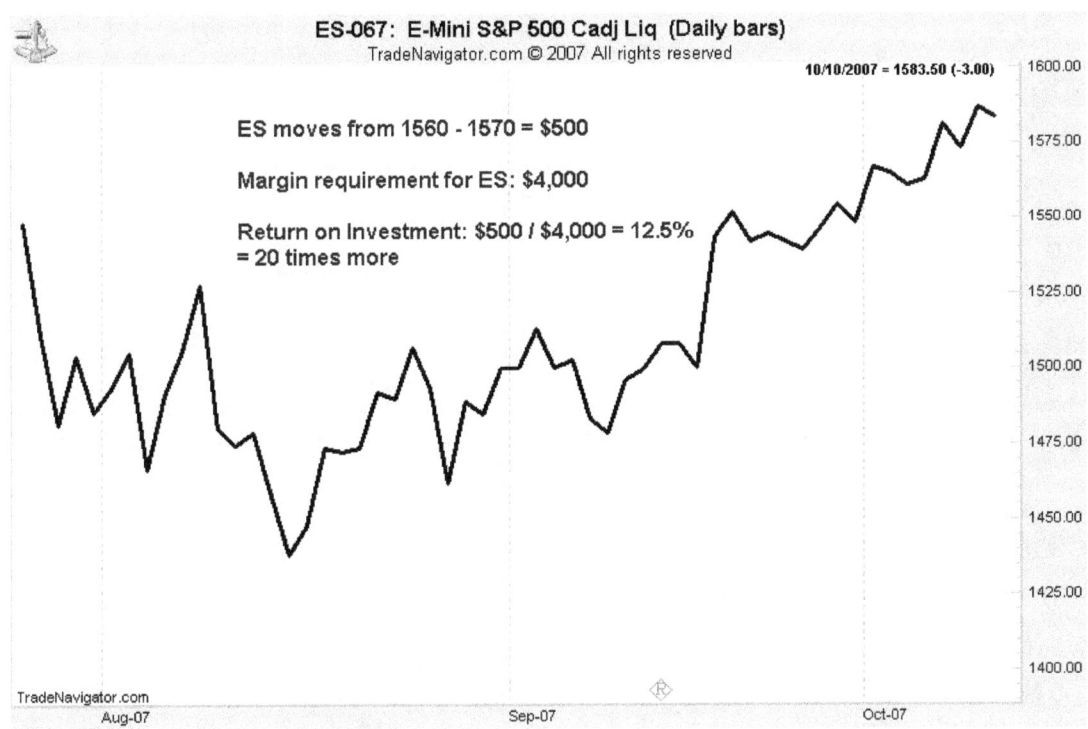

Of course, It can be a double-sided sword. You can easily **make** 500 dollars, but if the trade goes against you, you will **lose** 500 dollars. Trading one contract of the E-mini S&P is no different from trading 500 shares of the SPY.

The Futures Trading Myth

As you can see at the bottom of the previous chart, there are small Rs. These Rs indicate expiration dates. A futures contract is only valid for a specific time. In the case of the E-mini S&P, a futures contract is valid for three months. You might know It concept from options. Options also have an expiration date.

After the expiration date, a new futures contract starts trading, and the old contract expires. You might have heard horror stories that you will have to take delivery if you are holding a position and the futures contract expires. So, according to these tales, if you are trading the grains – corn, for example – and the contract expires, you will get the corn delivered to your doorstep.

No! That will not happen!

It will happen: before the futures contract expires, your broker will contact you and send you some information. It will probably be something to the effect of, "Alright, in a couple of days, It futures contract will expire. We should get rid of It position or roll it over." Rollovers are when one contract expires, and the other contract starts trading. Your broker will take care of something, so you don't have to do anything on your end.

Your broker doesn't have any interest in you getting a physical delivery of corn, you don't have any interest in getting a physical delivery of corn, and it's unlikely that anyone else has any interest in you getting a physical delivery of corn either. So, don't believe these horror stories.

Just be accessible to your broker, and you shouldn't have any problems. Ensure that he has a number where you can be reached to inform you of what's going on.

A Little More On Futures

Let's go back to the S&P 500 Index. As you can see by the decimals in the following graph, it's trading at one-cent increments.

To make futures trading a little easier, it's been simplified even further. If you look at the following example, it's changing in quarter increments on the same right side. If the E-mini S&P futures contract moves from 1560 to 1570, you'll make or lose 500 dollars, depending on what kind of position you took. And if a 10 point move translates into a $500 gain or loss, then a 1 point move is worth $50.

When trading the e-mini S&P, the minimum tick movement (or minimum movement) is a quarter. So, you can see that it goes from 1550 to 1550 and a quarter, 1550 and a half, 1550 and three quarters, and then up to 1551. If the minimum movement is a quarter, then every tick move totals $12.50 (one-quarter of $50). Very easy. There are four quarters in one point, so you just have to divide the 50 dollars by four.

So, why is that important? Well, it's not really – all you need to know is that when trading one futures contract with anywhere between 2,000 to 4,000 dollars, you can make a return of 50 dollars per point. Keep in mind that you can also LOSE 50 dollars per issue.

Remember, the 2,000 to 4,000 dollars we're talking about is the initial margin, which is the sum of money that a customer like you must deposit with the brokerage firm for each futures contract that you buy or sell.

Now, just think about It for a minute: let's assume that you have an 80,000 dollar account – what can you do with it? Well, you could buy 500 shares of the SPY stock. Or you could trade 20 futures contracts in the E.S. If you choose to exchange the 20 futures contracts instead of the 500 SPY stock shares, you'll make 10,000 dollars! If you stick with the SPY shares, you'll only make 500 dollars per 10-point move.

You can see the difference. You get much more significant leverage on your account with futures trading, and higher power is precisely what will help you grow your account (as long as you know what you're doing).

Margins and Accounts

There are two types of margins. The **initial margin** (sometimes called the original margin) is the sum of money that the customer must deposit with the brokerage firm for each futures contract to be bought or sold.
Both buyer and seller pay the initial margin.

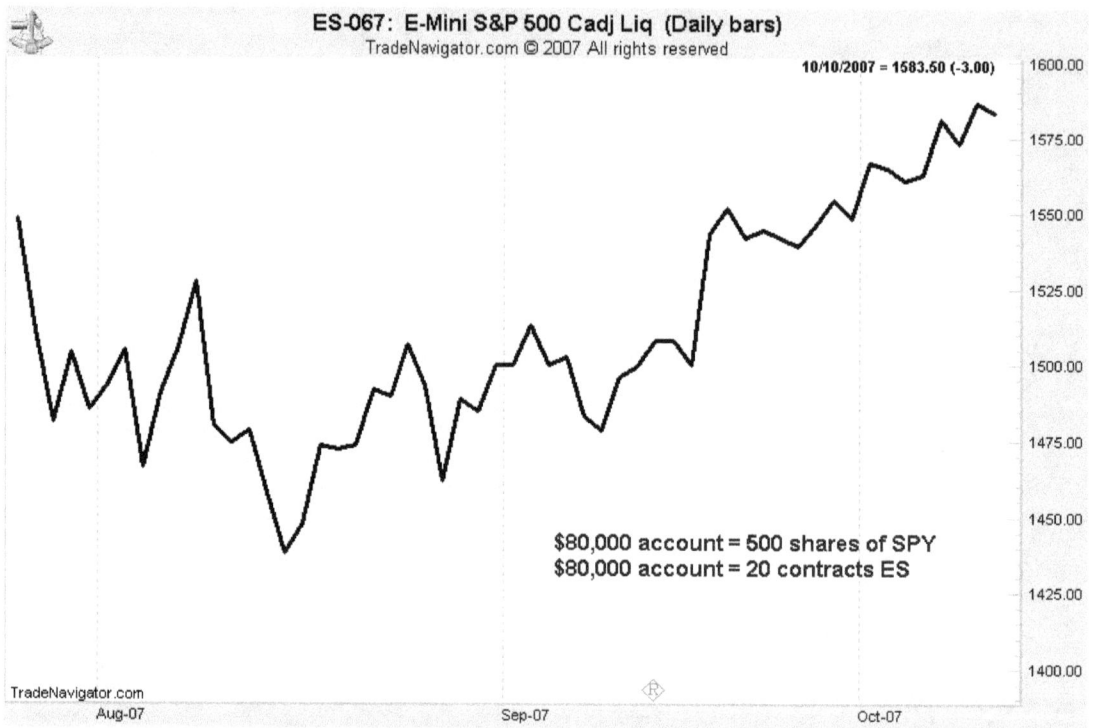

Additionally, the **maintenance margin** is the minimum amount an investor must keep on deposit in a margin account for each open contract. Typically, the maintenance margin is smaller than the initial margin. For example, Assume that the initial margin needed to buy or sell a particular futures contract is $2,000. A likely maintenance margin requirement might be $1,500.

Another essential thing to be aware of when dealing with margins is something called a **margin call.** Suppose the margin drops below the margin maintenance requirement established by the exchange listing the futures. In that case, a margin call will be issued to bring the account back up to the required level. If you need to have $1,500 in your account for your open contracts and don't, you can expect a margin call.

Another difference in trading futures vs. stocks is that your account is settled daily. Any day that profits accrue on your open positions, the profits will be added to the balance in your margin account automatically, not just when you close the position. When you are buying stocks, all the money that you make or lose will be either added or subtracted to your account <u>only</u> when you close the position.

So, when profits occur on your futures contracts, they will be added to the balance of your margin account, and on any day losses accrue, the losses will be deducted from the balance of your margin account.

Keep in mind, if the funds remaining in your margin account dip below the maintenance margin requirement, your broker will require that you deposit additional funds to bring the account back to the level of the required margin. Again, It is called a margin call.

Due to the low margin requirement, futures trading offers everyone an equal opportunity to make a fortune even with a small bank account.

Pros and Cons of Futures Trading

Futures trading is amongst today's most highly leveraged, potentially profitable financial pursuits. It allows traders to build up their accounts fast. But, as stated before, if you take futures trading lightly, you could also wipe out your trading account in days. Therefore, it's crucial to your trading success to diligently educate yourself in futures trading and trade only with a proven and reliable trading strategy.

If you're new to futures trading, it can be tough to decide WHICH contracts actually to trade. There are a lot of options! The best approach would probably be to start with the more popular commodities until you have a better idea of which contracts most fit you and your trading.

The more you know about the basics of futures contracts and commodities like It, the better your chances of trading success.

Let's check futures trading against our criteria:

1.) **Capital Requirements**

To trade a futures contract, you need to deposit an initial investment into your futures trading account. As of the book's writing, most futures brokers require a minimum of $5,000, though I have seen some brokers who are willing to open an account with as little as $2,000.

2.) **Leverage**

The leverage depends on the futures contract you're trading and the contract value. Each contract requires an initial margin. Here are some examples of the most popular agreements (as of January 2008):

E-mini S&P – as low as $500 to trade a $75,000 contract (Leverage 1:150)

E-mini N.Q. – as low as $500 to trade a $45,000 contract (Leverage 1:90)

E-mini gold – as low as $400 to trade a $27,000 contract (Leverage 1:67.5)

3.) **Liquidity**

Again, the liquidity depends on the futures contract you are trading. Here are some numbers:

E-mini S&P:	around 2,500,000 contracts/day
E-mini NQ:	around 500,000 contracts/day
Euro Currency:	around 200,000 contract/day

As you can see, the liquidity varies. Therefore you MUST check the volume of the futures market you are planning to trade.

4.) **Volatility**

You will find decent volatility in the futures markets. Like in the forex markets, the high leverage will allow you to make decent profits, even if the markets move just a few points.

Here are some average daily moves:

E-mini S&P:	between 1% and 3% per day
E-mini NQ:	between 1% and 2.5% per day
E-mini Gold:	between 1% and 2.5% per day
Euro Currency:	between 0.5% and 1.5% per day

Keep in mind that these moves represent approximately $500-$1,500 per day for each contract traded.

Conclusion:

Futures markets can be very liquid, and the capital requirements are as low as $2,000. The leverage is at least 1:50, and there's decent volatility.

Futures markets are regulated, and the spread is typically one tick (minimum movement of the contract). Commissions are usually below $5 per transaction. It's no surprise that many day traders choose the futures market for their trading endeavors.

Ensure the market volume and liquidity you want to trade since there are huge differences between the markets.

Trading Stock Options

Stock options trading is quite similar to futures trading – they both involve the process of buying stocks at a pre-determined price and then selling them when the price rises above its original amount.

When you buy an option, you have the right – but not the obligation – to buy (call) or sell (put) a specific underlying asset at a prearranged price on or before a given date.

Example:

Let's assume that you buy a call – a right to buy – 100 shares of ACME Holding Inc. at an agreed price of $40 per share (strike price), on an agreed date in March of 2008 (expiration date), and you pay $5 for the option.

If on – or before – the expiration date, ACME Holding Inc. is trading at less than $40 per share, then you would not exercise your option, and you would have lost the price you paid on that option – $5.

But, if ACME Holding, Inc. is trading at $50 per share on or before the expiration date, your option is, in effect, worth $10. The difference between the price your chance to buy ACME Holding, Inc. is set at – in It case, $40 – and the price at which it is trading – $50.

The reverse of It is a put (right to sell) option on an underlying asset. You might feel that the market is overheated at present, and you want to buy a put (right to sell) option.

It will give the individual who bought the put option the right to sell that option at an agreed-upon price (strike price) on or before a specific date (expiration date).

> A Little Bit of History
>
> Options are one of the oldest trading vehicles that man has ever used. Around 600 B.C., Thales used the stars to predict that there would be a bumper olive harvest, and he bought options on the use of olive presses. When the harvest did, prove to be a great one, Thales was able to rent the presses out at a significant profit.

Let's check stock options trading against our criteria:

1.) Capital Requirements

Like stock trading, day trading stock options is subject to the Pattern Day Trading Rule introduced by the NYSE and NASD in August and September of 2001. It rules dictates that "if a trader executes four or more day trades within a five-business-day period, then he must maintain a minimum equity of $25,000 in his margin account at all times." It means that you need at least $28,000-$30,000 if you want to day trade stock options since you need some money to buy votes.

2.) Leverage

The leverage depends on the option you choose. Without going into too much detail, the price for the choice depends on the time until expiration, the volatility of the underlying stock, and the "inner value" – i.e., if the option is already "in the money."

Nevertheless, you will notice that options offer the high leverage.

Example: On December 27, 2007, IBM was trading at $110.16 per share. If you wanted to buy 100 shares of IBM, you would have had to invest $11,016. The January Call, at a strike price of $110, with 23 days left to expiration, only cost $3.30, and you could buy the right to purchase 100 IBM shares within the next 23 days for only $330.

In It example, the leverage is approximately 1:30.

3.) **Liquidity**

Options are typically not very liquid. Even if you trade options on the Dow 30 stocks, you will notice that only a few thousand possibilities are sold per day. The reason for the low volume is the broad choice of options. At any given time, you have several strike prices and multiple expiration dates available.

Fortunately, option prices are NOT subject to market manipulation since the value of an option is not determined by supply and demand but by a mathematical formula created by Black and Scholes. But you do have a significant spread between the bid and the ask; in our IBM example, $0.10 or 3% of the option price.

4.) **Volatility**

Options that are traded "at the money" or "in the money" typically have very high volatility. We chose an IBM "at the money" option with 23 days to expiration in our example. The current price was $3.30, and throughout the day, it was trading as high as $3.95. The previous day's close was $4.30.

Therefore, the intraday volatility for the It option was almost 20%. Considering the last day's close, the overall volatility was close to 30%.

Conclusion

Stock options trading offers similar advantages and disadvantages to stock trading – you need a minimum of $25,000 in your trading account if you want to day trade stock options. The leverage is higher than when you're trading stocks but much lower than trading futures or forex. The liquidity is very low compared to the other markets, and the volatility is scary.

Stock options are a fantastic instrument to trade when traded on daily or weekly charts. Day trading stock options is hazardous and challenging, and not for the novice trader.

Action Items:

Decide which market you want to trade. Spend four more hours learning about the market you choose. Surf the Internet and read articles. Try to find out as much as you can about your preferred market without being overloaded with information.

Continue your trading plan on page 245 and fill in the market you selected under "Selecting a Market."

Step 2: Selecting a Timeframe

When day trading, you'll select a timeframe that is less than one day. Popular intraday timeframes are 60-minute, 30-minute, 15-minute, 10minute, 5-minute, 3-minute, and 1-minute.

When you select a smaller timeframe (less than 60 minutes), your average profit per trade is usually relatively low. On the other hand, you get more trading opportunities. When trading on a larger timeframe, your average profit per transaction will be more significant, but you'll have fewer trading opportunities.

Smaller timeframes mean smaller profits, but usually smaller risk, too. When you're starting with a small trading account, you might want to select a short timeframe to make sure you're not over-leveraging your account.

However, when selecting a minimal timeframe like 1-minute, 3minute, or 5-minute, you might experience a lot of "noise" caused by hedge funds, scalpers, and automated trading.

You might think that you see an emerging trend to realize that it was only a short manipulated move and that the movement is over as soon as you enter the market.

Therefore I recommend using 15-minute charts. It timeframe is small enough for you to capture the nice intraday moves, but it's big enough to eliminate the noise in the market and correctly displays the
"true trends."

When developing a trading strategy, you should always experiment with different timeframes. A trading strategy that doesn't work on a small timetable might work on a larger timeframe and vice versa.

Start developing your trading strategy using 15-minute charts. If you're unhappy with the results, change the timeframe before changing the entry or exit rules.

Action Items:

Continue your trading plan on page 245 and select an initial timeframe for yourself under "Selecting a Timeframe."

Step 3: Selecting a Trading Approach

After selecting a market, you need to decide which trading approach you would like to use. The main question is whether you'll use fundamental or technical analysis to determine which instrument to trade and when to enter and exit.

Fundamental Analysis

Let's take a look at the definition of fundamental analysis:

> *"Fundamental stock analysis requires, among other things, a close examination of the financial statements for the company to determine its current financial strength, future growth and profitability prospects, and current management skills, to estimate whether the stock's price is undervalued or overvalued. A good deal of reliance is placed on annual and quarterly earnings reports, the economic, political and competitive environment facing the company, as well as any current news items or rumors relating to the company's operations."*

Source: www.daytrading.about.com

In other words, fundamental analysis is the study of primary, underlying factors that affect the supply and demand of the contracts which are being traded. Fundamental analysis looks at the CAUSE of market movement.

In the following graph, you'll find a snapshot of some "key statistics" for IBM. In addition to It company-specific data, you need to consider the overall economic environment and start looking at various macroeconomic indicators, such as economic growth rates, interest rates, inflation rates, and unemployment rates.

As an example, interest rate hikes are seldom good news for stock markets. Many investors will withdraw money from a country's stock market when there is a hike in interest rates, causing the country's currency to weaken.

Knowing which effect prevails can be tricky. When the Fed announced an interest rate cut in December of 2007, the Dow Jones Index dropped 300 points. When the Fed cut interest rates in January of 2008, the Dow Jones Index jumped 200 points.

Besides, economic reports with crucial data like the PPI, CPI, PMI, GDP, and, recently, even housing statistics have proven to have a significant impact on the stock market.

Confused? If the abbreviations and the "key statistics" on the following graph don't make sense to you, or if they confuse you, then you are not alone.

Fundamental analysis is not easy. That's why most market analysts have some background in economics, both macro-, and microeconomics. Big trading companies like Goldman Sachs are employing analysts with Ph. D.s in economics, and you shouldn't try to compete with them.

Even if you decide NOT to trade stocks and want to focus on futures or the forex market, then you still need to take a look at crop and weather reports (if you are trading grain futures), interest rates, and the country's economic data (if you are trading forex), or follow developments in the Middle East and the status of the pipelines and refineries all over the world (if you are trading energy futures).

Key Statistics

Data provided by Capital IQ, except where noted.

Get Key Statistics for: IBM

VALUATION MEASURES	
Market Cap (intraday)[5]:	173.11B
Enterprise Value (27-Dec-07)[3]:	175.22B
Trailing P/E (ttm, intraday):	16.22
Forward P/E (fye 31-Dec-08)[1]:	13.73
PEG Ratio (5 yr expected):	1.48
Price/Sales (ttm):	1.87
Price/Book (mrq):	5.83
Enterprise Value/Revenue (ttm)[3]:	1.82
Enterprise Value/EBITDA (ttm)[3]:	9.174

FINANCIAL HIGHLIGHTS	
Fiscal Year	
Fiscal Year Ends:	31-Dec
Most Recent Quarter (mrq):	30-Sep-07
Profitability	
Profit Margin (ttm):	10.40%
Operating Margin (ttm):	14.49%
Management Effectiveness	
Return on Assets (ttm):	8.19%
Return on Equity (ttm):	36.25%
Income Statement	
Revenue (ttm):	96.18B
Revenue Per Share (ttm):	66.152
Qtrly Revenue Growth (yoy):	6.60%
Gross Profit (ttm):	38.30B
EBITDA (ttm):	19.10B
Net Income Avl to Common (ttm):	9.93B
Diluted EPS (ttm):	6.76
Qtrly Earnings Growth (yoy):	6.30%
Balance Sheet	
Total Cash (mrq):	13.82B
Total Cash Per Share (mrq):	10.032
Total Debt (mrq):	35.32B
Total Debt/Equity (mrq):	1.719
Current Ratio (mrq):	1.035

TRADING INFORMATION	
Stock Price History	
Beta:	1.63
52-Week Change[3]:	14.77%
S&P500 52-Week Change[3]:	4.96%
52-Week High (11-Oct-07)[3]:	121.46
52-Week Low (01-Mar-07)[3]:	88.77
50-Day Moving Average[3]:	106.46
200-Day Moving Average[3]:	111.17
Share Statistics	
Average Volume (3 month)[3]:	7,982,700
Average Volume (10 day)[3]:	7,093,690
Shares Outstanding[5]:	1.58B
Float:	1.38B
% Held by Insiders[1]:	0.05%
% Held by Institutions[1]:	64.40%
Shares Short (as of 09-Nov-07)[3]:	13.24M
Short Ratio (as of 09-Nov-07)[3]:	1.5
Short % of Float (as of 09-Nov-07)[3]:	1.00%
Shares Short (prior month)[3]:	13.83M
Dividends & Splits	
Forward Annual Dividend Rate[4]:	1.60
Forward Annual Dividend Yield[4]:	1.40%
Trailing Annual Dividend Rate[3]:	1.50
Trailing Annual Dividend Yield[3]:	1.30%
5 Year Average Dividend Yield[4]:	0.80%
Payout Ratio[4]:	21%
Dividend Date[3]:	10-Dec-07
Ex-Dividend Date[4]:	07-Nov-07
Last Split Factor (new per old)[2]:	2:1
Last Split Date[3]:	27-May-99
Forward Annual Dividend Rate[4]:	1.60

Technical Analysis

Here is how technical analysis is defined:

> "The necessary foundations or premises of technical analysis are that

a stock's current price discounts all information available in the market, those price movements are not random and that patterns in price movements, in very many cases, tend to repeat themselves or trend in some direction.

Therefore technical analysis involves the study of a stock's trading patterns through the use of charts, trendlines, support and resistance levels, and many other mathematical analysis tools, to predict future movements in a stock's price and to help identify trading opportunities."

Source: www.daytrading.about.com

In summary, there are three main points that a technical analyst applies:

1.) Market action discounts everything. Regardless of what the fundamentals are saying, the price you see is the price you get.

2.) The price of a given security moves in trends.

3.) The historical trading patterns of a security will tend to repeat.

All three of the points above are essential, but the first is the most critical. You must understand It moment because it's the basis of our trading approach.

When you look at any financial instrument's price as a technical analyst, you believe that it's the instrument's real value as the market sees it.

I believe in technical analysis for a couple of reasons.

1.) The markets are driven by greed and fear and not by supply and demand. An economic report itself is meaningless: traders' reactions to the information that moves the market.

Price data is more "objective." You can interpret financial data and economic reports any way you want. Still, support levels are support levels, and a weekly high is a weekly high. It's easier to interpret hard facts than financial statements because, many times, these statements might be misleading.

Example: IBM announces that it will meet the projected sales targets, and the shares drop like a rock because traders hoped that IBM would exceed its goals. Another day, DELL announces that they will meet their targets. The shares jump up because traders didn't believe that DELL would make it due to the "difficult economic environment."

2.) It's easier (and therefore faster) to learn technical analysis. You can learn the basics by reading a couple of books. In contrast, you need to study micro-and macro-economics to master fundamental analysis. And even then, you might be fooled by the market.

An Example Of How Fundamental Analysis Can Fool You

On Friday, April 7th, 2006, the unemployment rate for March was published. The market expected an unemployment rate of 4.8%, and the numbers came in better than expected.

Only 4.7%. That's good news, isn't it? The market should move up, right? WRONG! On that day the E-mini S&P dropped 20 points. Why? Well, here are some comments from a news service:

"Not surprisingly, Friday's equity trade was dictated by the March employment report. More specifically, it was the Treasury market's reaction to it that set the stage for stocks."

"A lack of negative surprise caused the stock market to breathe a sigh of relief."

"The Treasury market had a very divergent reaction to the data, and it took the stock market down with it. For Treasury traders, the in-line data essentially provided no evidence that the Fed will be inclined to soon end its monetary tightening cycle."

Oops. So the stock traders thought there was good news and the market was moving up, but the treasury trader in the other room thought the unemployment data was bad news. So treasury

Using a technical approach, you don't have to twist your mind to come up with an explanation for why the market behaves as it does. You simply believe that the factors which affect the price – including fundamental, political, and psychological factors – have all been built into the price you see.

It means that anything that can affect a financial instrument's price has already been factored into the market participants' current price. Technical analysts look at charts the same way a doctor would look at x-rays: they examine the charts for information on the markets' future direction.

Day Trading Charts

If you're new to the trading game and not a Ph.D. in Economics, then charts are the way to go. The most basic charts are bar and line charts. Even if you're an experienced trader, bar and line maps probably still have a special place in your daily trading life. These charts are indispensable.

"A picture speaks a thousand words." It proverb holds just as right for charts. Charting is the graphical expression of a financial market's behavior over a while.

Any market has four different trading points throughout one day. They are opening price (O), closing price (C), the high total cost of the day (H), and the low total price of the day (L). All of these points appear on the charts.

The opening price (O) is the first trade of the day. Individual traders tend to place orders when the market opens, in reaction to the previous day's close. Its price will usually be based on emotional decisions. It could well indicate how the first half – or the whole day's trading – will pan out.

The closing price (C) is the last trade of the day. It is generally institutional investors that place orders towards the day's close. Unlike the opening price, the closing price will generally represent reason and research decisions – not gut feel.

The day's low (L) and the day's high (H) are pretty self-explanatory. The difference between the high and low on the charts is referred to as the Range.

The fifth variable displayed on a chart is typically the volume (V), specifying the number of shares, lots, or contracts traded during the time between the open market and the close.

Purely looking at these five points on the charts will not be enough to plan future trades. You need to look at them over a series of times to evaluate trends in the market.

Day traders use trading charts to watch the markets they trade and decide when to make their trades. There are several different types of trading charts. Still, they all show essentially the same trading information, such as the past and current prices.

In the following section, we'll discuss the three most popular types of trading charts.

Bar Charts

A bar chart, also known as a bar graph, is a chart with rectangular bars whose lengths are proportional to the value they represent. Bar charts are used for comparing two or more values.

The bar chart is one of the most common charting methods. A bar chart indicates a single bar that extends from the high to the low of the trading period it is meant to depict. Besides, the opening and closing price levels could be displayed as small branches coming from the main bar at the appropriate level. Closing prices are put on the right side of the bar. Opening prices are set on the left side.

How to Read Bar Charts

Bar charts consist of an opening foot, a vertical line, and a closing foot. Each bar includes the open, high, low, and close of the timeframe and also shows the direction (upward or downward) and the range of the timeframe.

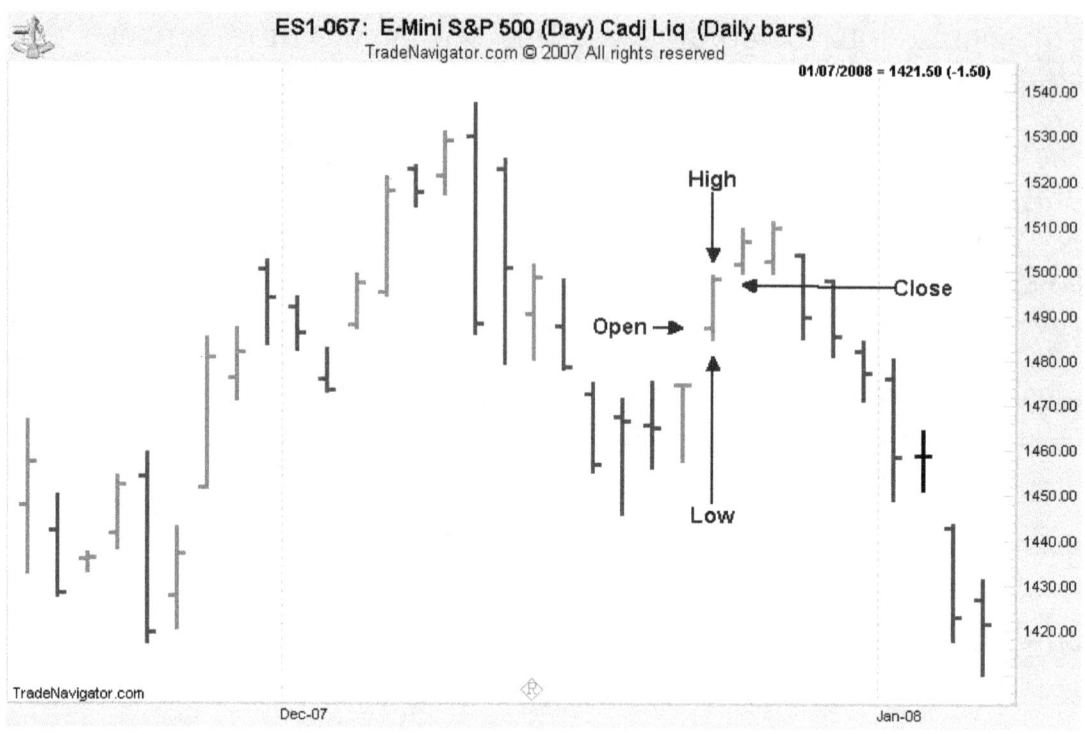

During live trading, you can read the bar chart like It:

1.) **Open** – The open is the first price traded during the bar and is indicated by the flat foot on the bar's left side.

2.) **High** – The high is the highest price traded during the bar and is indicated by the top of the vertical bar.

3.) **Low** – The low is the lowest price traded during the bar and is indicated by the vertical bar's bottom.

4.) **Close** – The close is the last price traded during the bar and is indicated by the horizontal foot on the bar's right side.

5.) **Direction** – The direction of the bar is indicated by the locations of the opening and closing feet. If the closing foot is above the opening foot, the bar is an upward bar, and if the closing foot is below the opening foot, the bar is low. Sometimes a charting software allows you to color these bars, in which case the upward bars are typically colored green, and the low bars are colored red.

6.) **Range** – The bar's scope is indicated by the locations of the top and bottom of the bar. The content is calculated by subtracting the low from the high (range = high - low).

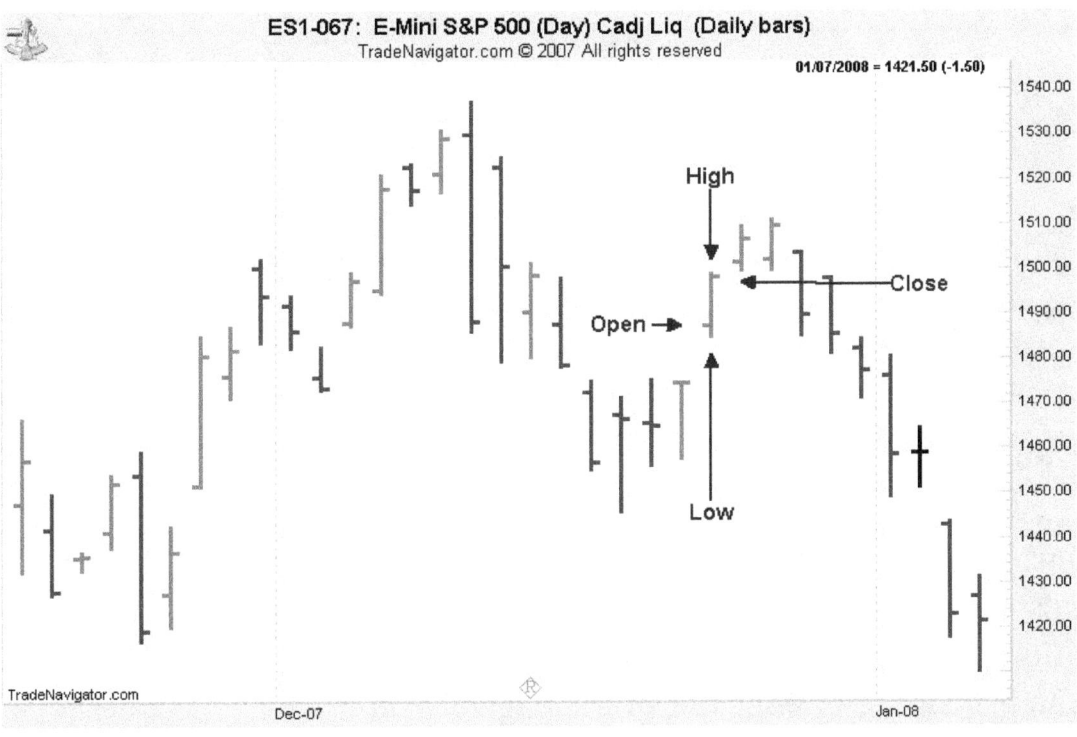

Candlestick Charts

Candlestick charts are not new – they've been used for hundreds of years by Japanese traders to predict and act on market movements.

Candlestick charting gives greater insight into human psychology.

In the 1700s, Homma, a Japanese trader in rice, noticed how the price of rice was influenced by human psychology as much as by the supply and demand situation. Homma used candlestick charts to trade rice and amassed a considerable fortune in the markets. It was rumored that he never had a single losing trade!

Human psychology has never changed; it has remained constant over time – candlestick charting is just as useful today as it was hundreds of years ago.

Even though they may look a little complicated, there are some great reasons to use candlestick charts. Here are the main ones:

1.) **Complement Other Technical Tools**

You can use candlestick charts to use the standard bar chart, and you can combine them with traditional market indicators. Candlestick charts are a great way to spot opportunities, filter, and time trades with other hands.

2.) **Spotting Trend Changes**

Because of how candlestick charts are viewed, they can give you visual warnings of market reversals much more clearly than traditional bar charts. If you look at candlestick charting, the move's human psychology jumps out of the page at you.

3.) **Straightforward to Use**

Candlestick charts use the same open, high, low, and close data that traditional bar charts use and are easy to draw. The different candle names are also easy to remember.

4.) **Define Market Momentums**

The candlestick chart is drawn the direction of the price and the momentum behind the move.

How to Read Candlestick Charts

Candlestick charts consist of a broad vertical line and a narrow vertical tube. Each candlestick includes the open, high, low, and close of the timeframe, the direction (upward or downward) of the timeframe, and the range of the timeframe.

During live trading, you can read the candlestick chart like It:

1.) **Open** – The open is the first price traded during the candlestick. It is indicated by either the top or bottom of the broad vertical line (the base for an upward candlestick and the top for a downward candlestick).

2.) **High** – The high is the highest price traded during the candlestick and is indicated by the top of the thin vertical bar (the candlestick's wick).

3.) **Low** – The low is the lowest price traded during the candlestick. It is indicated by the thin vertical bar (the upside-down the wick of the candlestick).

4.) **Close** – The close is the last price traded during the candlestick. It is indicated by either the top or bottom of the broad vertical line (the top for an upward candlestick and a downward candlestick).

5.) **Direction** – The candlestick's path is indicated by the candlestick's color (specifically the broad vertical line). Usually, if the candlestick is green, the candlestick is an upward candlestick. If the candlestick is red, the candlestick is downward, but these colors can be customized. In the following chart, the upward candlesticks are colored black, and the low candlesticks are colored white.

6.) **Range** – The candlestick range is indicated by the top and bottom of the thin vertical lines (the wicks). The content is calculated by subtracting the low from the high (range = high - low).

The candlestick chart body graphically illustrates the relationship behind the open, high, low, and close. It adds an extra visual edge due to the way they're drawn.

The candlestick has a wide part, called the "real body." It real body represents the range between the open and close of that day's trading.

If the real body is filled with red, it means the close was lower than the open. If the natural body is green, it means the opposite – the finish was higher than the open.

Above and below the real body, we see the "shadows." We see these as the wicks of the candle (which give them their name). The shadows show the high and the low of the day's trading.

If the upper shadow on the green filled-in body is short, it indicates that the open day was closer to the day's high. On the other hand, a short upper shadow on a red or unfilled body shows the close was near the high.

Regardless of whether you're a day trader, a position trader, a system trader, or a trader who likes to make your trades, there's nothing to dislike about candlestick charts.

They're comfortable, and they're fun to use. Plus, they provide greater insight into market moves and the versatility to be used in any trading. If you aren't already using candlestick charting, then it's time to start.

Line Charts

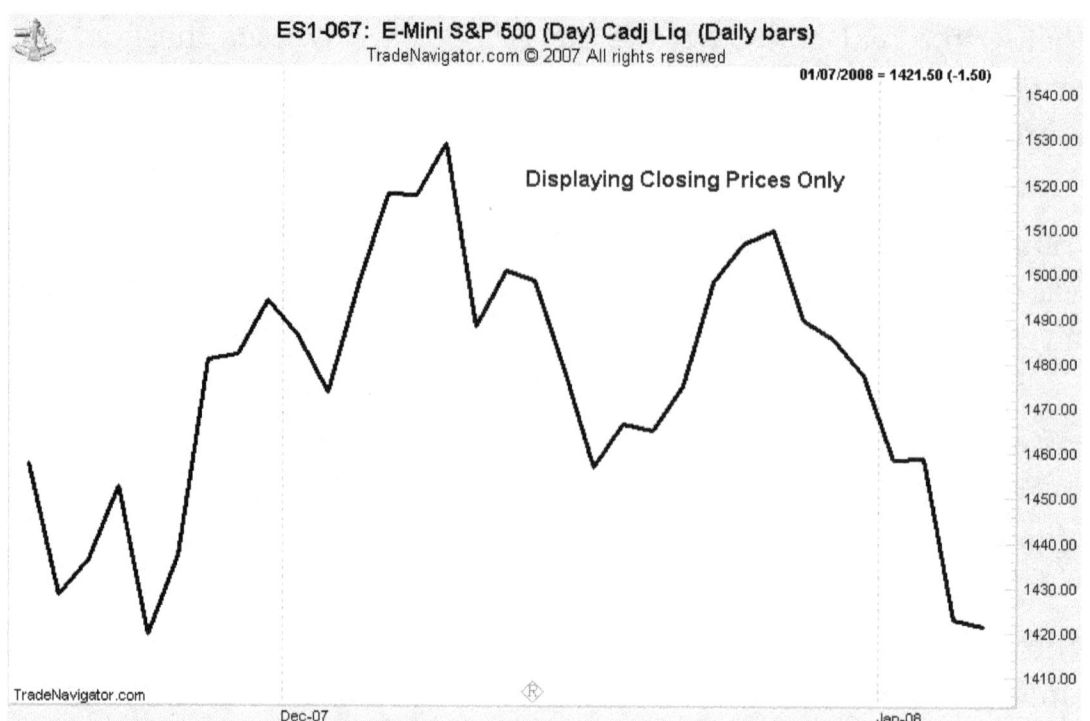

A simple line chart draws a line from one closing price to the next closing price. Line charts show the general price movement over some time. Some investors and traders consider the closing level more important than the open, high, or low. By paying attention to only the close, intraday swings can be ignored.

Line charts are also used when open, high, and low data points are not available. Sometimes only the closing data is available for individual indices, thinly traded stocks, and intraday prices.

How to Read Line Charts

Line charts consist of individual points that are connected with straight lines. Usually, each point shows the timeframe's close, but It can be modified to show any info – open, high, or low. Line charts also show the direction (upward or downward) of the timeframe.

Using Charts In Your Trading

Most charting software supports bar, candlestick, and line charts. Usually, you can customize the display and colors according to your wish.

You can use any reliable online charting service you want. Just make sure they provide the necessary analytical tools (e.g., the capability to draw trendlines and the option to add moving averages). There are so many charting services out there that it would be hard to mention anyone in particular.

Let's just put it It way: charts are not the crystal ball of trading.

Charts do not foretell future market behaviors or predict market prices. They offer you a concise and accurate history of the price movements of a particular market. In that history lays a trend. You can extrapolate data to base your future projections of probable market behaviors and price changes from its direction. That's the most outstanding value that you'll get when it comes to using charts.

Technical Indicators

Let's keep it simple: money is made if you buy when the market is going up and sell when the market is going down. That's why technical analysts hold to the motto "the trend is your friend."

Finding the prevailing trend will help you become aware of the overall market direction and offer you better visibility – especially when short term movements tend to clutter the picture.

Trends

The price chart of a security may appear like a random distribution, but It is not so.

About 30% of the time, security will be in a definite trend. The rest of the time, prices will trade more or less in a sideways range. Our job is to recognize trends early, emerge from non-trends, or as reversals of prior trends.

Our goal is to buy or sell our security early in these new trends, exiting the trade profitably when the movement ends. Its identification of activity, both its beginning and end, is the most important task we have as traders.

A simple definition of a trend is the general direction of price movements. An uptrend is present when prices make a series of higher highs and higher lows. A downtrend is current when prices make a series of lower highs and lower lows.

When prices move without such a discernible series, prices are trading sideways in a range of trading trend-less. Once a trend is noticeable, then trendlines can be drawn to define the lower limits of an uptrend or the upper limits.

Trendlines must be drawn correctly. It recognizes the trendline and the violation of Its trendline, which is your key to successful trading and fortune building.

Does All of It Sound Too Simple?

I know that these simple definitions sound mundane. Many traders would like to jump right into complicated indicators and complex trading strategies. Don't make It mistake.

Trading can be simple: you buy when the market is going up and sell when the market goes down. That's how money is made. But if you don't know HOW to recognize when the market is going up and when it's going down, then you'll lose money very quickly. So you MUST find an easy way to identify the direction of the market.

The easiest way to do so is using trend lines. Indicators are another way to determine the direction of the market. Still, suppose you learn how to identify the trend using simple trend lines. In that case, you'll never have to worry about indicators again.

The only two questions that remain are:

  * When should I enter? When should I exit?

Just keep reading for the answers.

Uptrend

Let me show you exactly how to draw a trend line. The following chart is a 5-minute bar chart of the E-mini S&P. The trading day is December 20, 2007.

As you can see, prices have been moving down all morning, and then they started moving sideways during the lunch break.

At 11:50 pm (Central Standard Time), we see the low of the day.

Prices have found resistance at 1462.50, and at 12:25 pm, prices break resistance on high volume. Prices are now in an uptrend, and it's time to draw our trendline.

In an uptrend, trendlines are drawn <u>below</u> the prices, while in a downtrend, trendlines are drawn <u>above</u> the costs.

To draw a line, we need two points. The first point is the low of the day and the second point is the first retracement when prices are no longer making higher lows.

The first time prices are not making a higher low occurs at the 12:15 pm bar, and we can draw our trendline. The dark part of the line is the **confirmed trend,** and the light part of the line is the **projected trend**.

At 12:35 pm, we see a lower low in an upward trend for the second time, but we do NOT adjust the trendline. **As a rule, trendlines can only become flatter, not steeper.** Adjusting the second lower low trend would make a steeper trendline; therefore, no change is made.

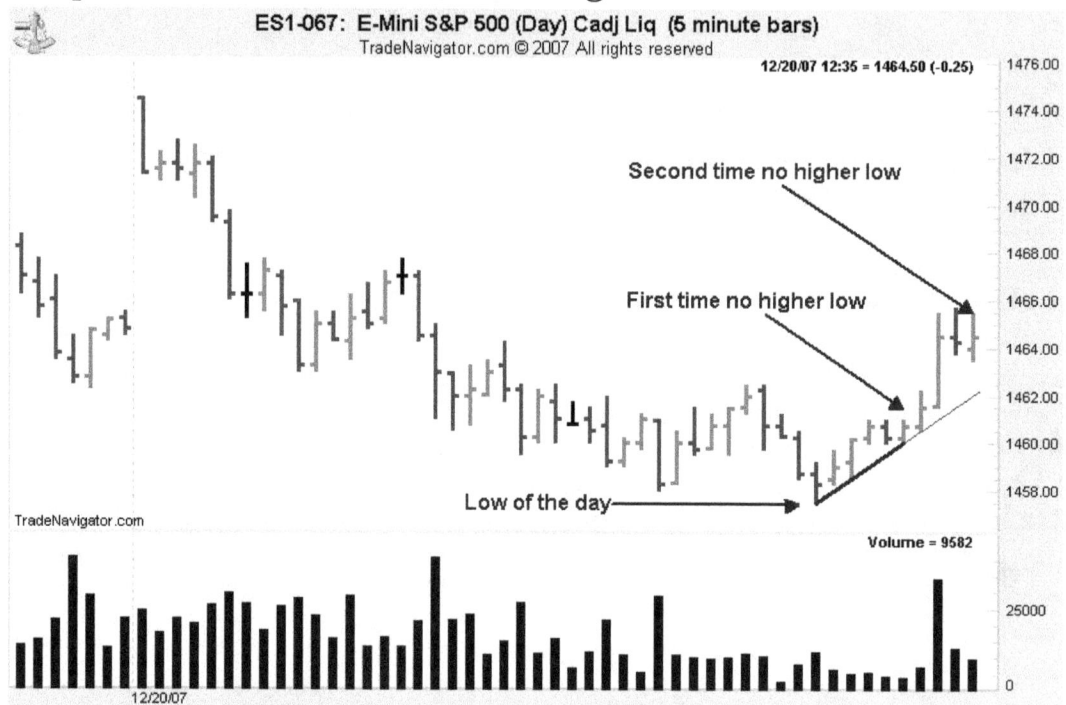

At 12:45 pm and 12:50 pm, a lower low is made again, and It time we adjust the trendline. It's only a slight adjustment, and the trendline becomes a little bit flatter. All previous prices are above the trendline, so the trend is still intact.

The next lower low occurs at 1:05 pm, and we can extend our trendline. It's a simple extension: no adjustment is needed. We see that the uptrend has now been in place for 40 minutes since the breakout through the resistance level at 1462.50 at 12:25 pm.

Ten minutes later, we get the next lower low, and we adjust the trendline accordingly. See how beautifully the previous lower lows are almost touching the trendline? A perfect trend.

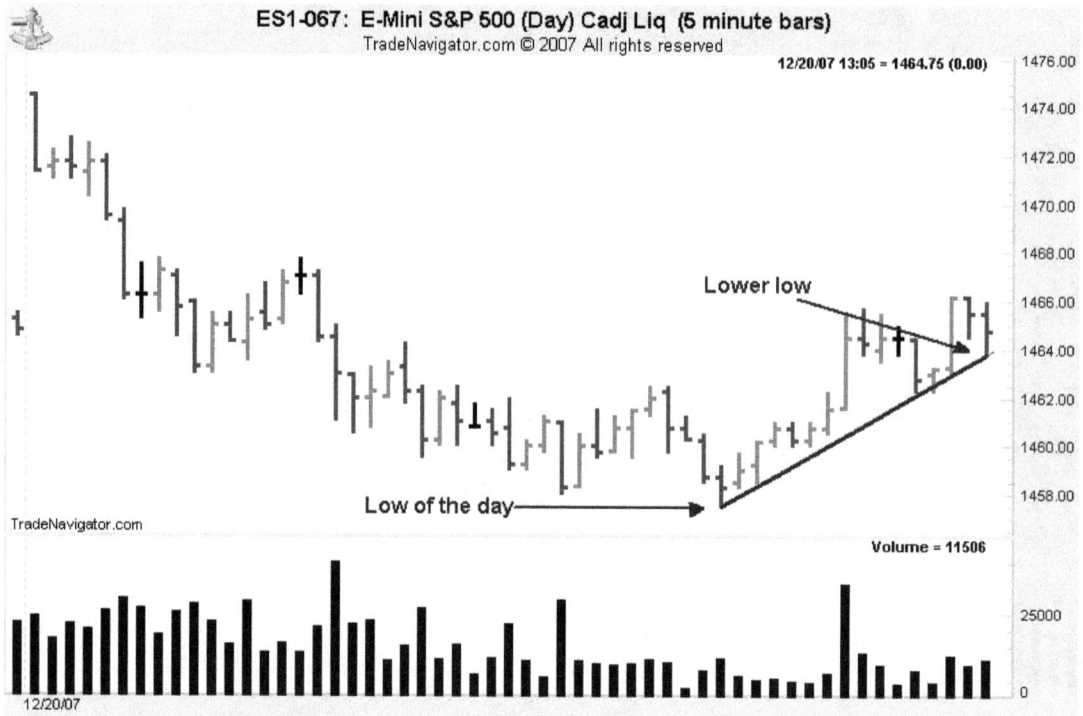

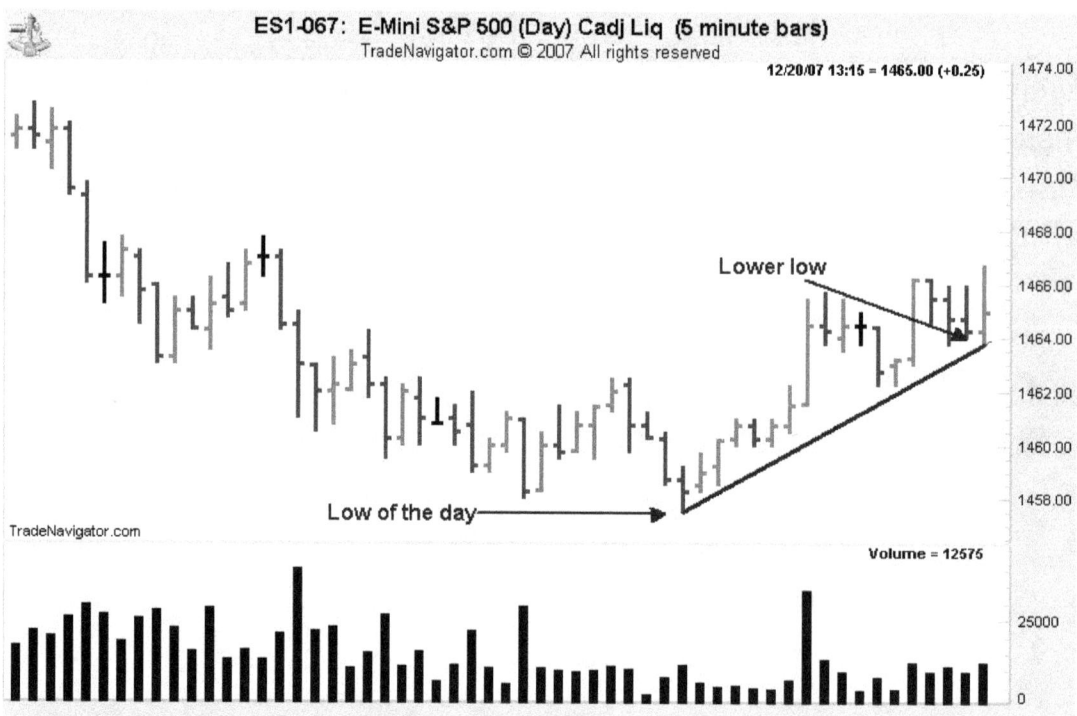

Again we see a lower low, but we don't adjust the trendline since it would make the line steeper. Remember the rule: we can only flatten the line. We can't make it steeper.

Another lower low occurs at 1:50 pm, but we don't adjust the trendline.

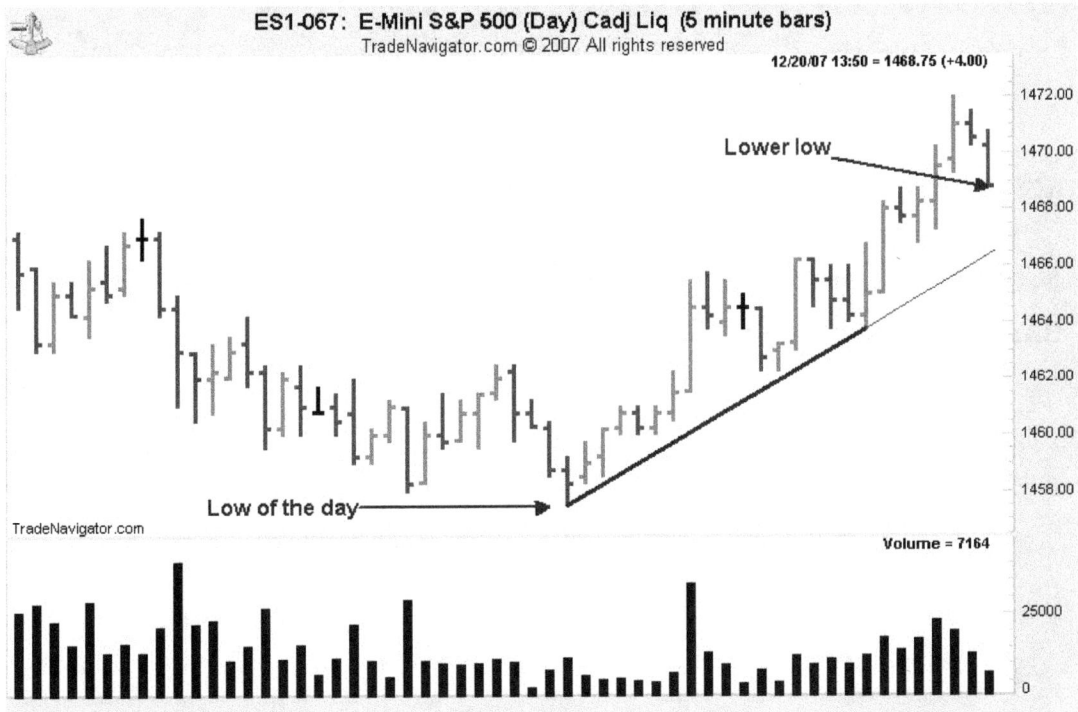

In It next chart, we see a series of lower lows, but only the lower low at 2:05 pm allows us to adjust the trendline. The series of lower lows indicates that the trend is coming to an end.

Fifteen minutes later, we have another lower low. Still, at the same time, we are experiencing a higher high after a series of lower highs. Lower highs indicate a possible downtrend, and when we see the first higher high, it's time to start drawing a **downtrend line**.

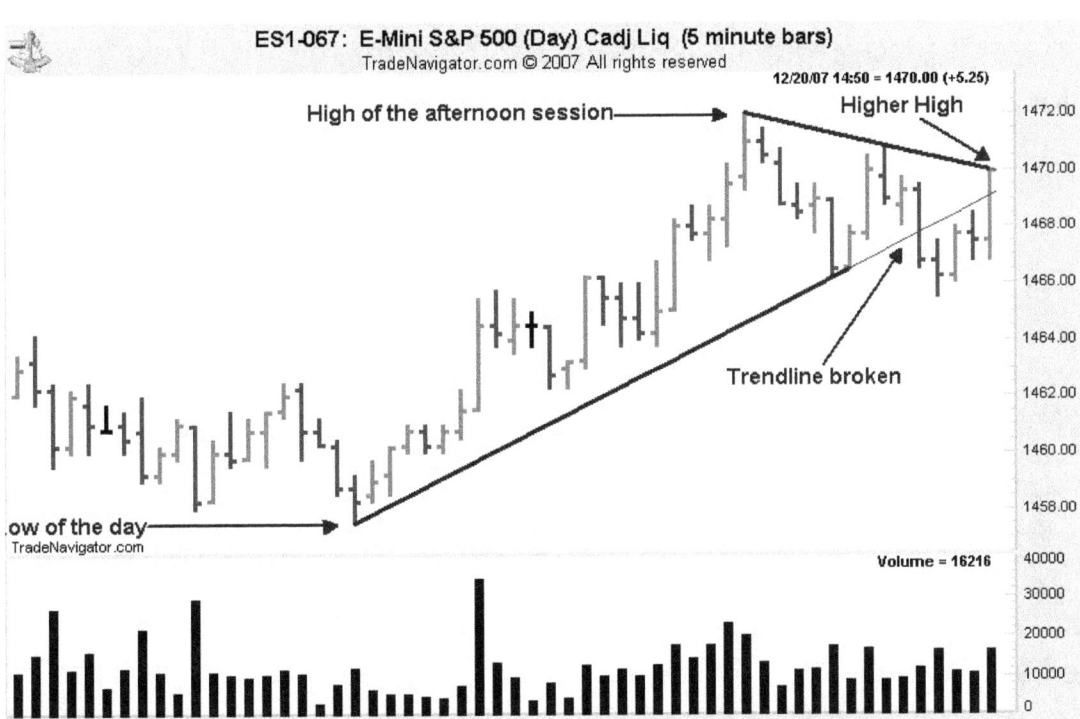

It seems that our uptrend has come to an end. The uptrend line is broken, and we have another higher high that confirms our downtrend line.

The uptrend was in place from 12:25 pm until 2:25 pm, for a full two hours. During It time, prices moved from 1462.50 (a break through the resistance level) to a high of 1472. The uptrend was broken at 1467.75.

There are two key things to remember about trendlines:

    1.)   **Never adjust a trendline so that it becomes steeper.**

    Don't run a trendline through price bars. An uptrend line is always below the price bars.

2.)   Keep a trendline close to the lower lows, and don't move it too far away.

If there's too much distance between your line and the lower lows, you risk missing a change in the trend.

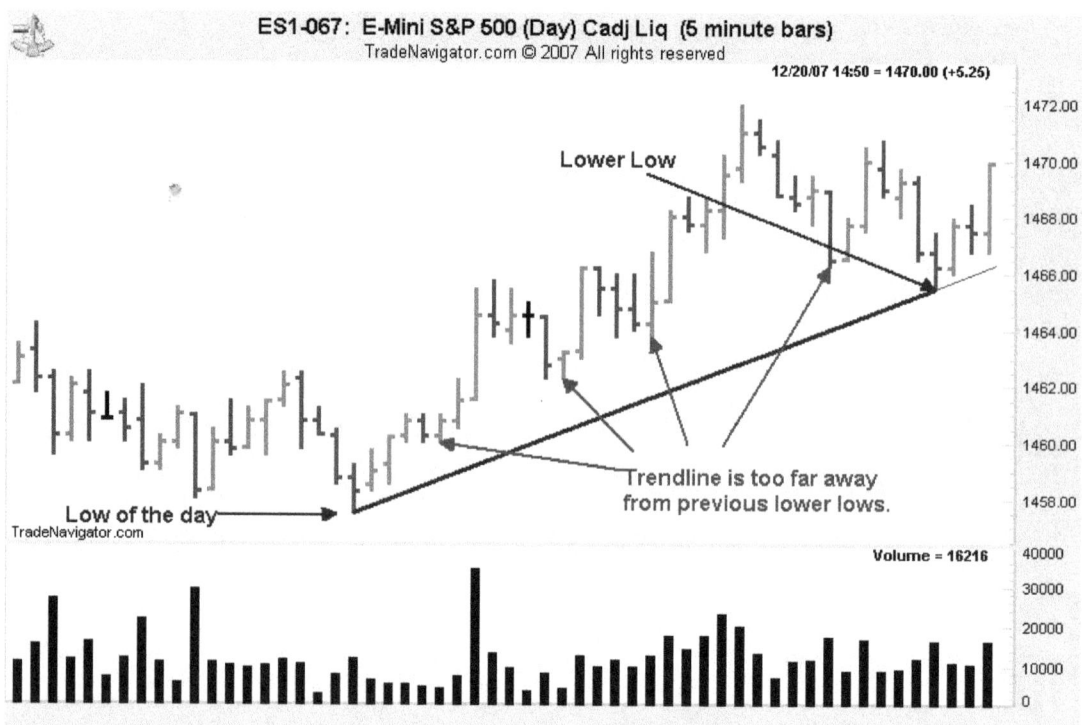

Downtrend

A downtrend line is constructed in a similar way to that of the uptrend line. The main difference is that you're looking for a higher high, and you draw the trendline ABOVE the price bars.

Here we had a 5-minute chart of the E-mini S&P on December 20, 2007. The opening price is also the highest, and 15 minutes after the opening, at 8:45 am, we have the first higher high. So we can draw our downtrend line.

The market keeps falling, and at 9:10 am, we see the next higher high. However, we don't adjust the trendline since it would mean making the line steeper.

We see another higher high at 9:35 am, but we still don't adjust the trendline. The 9:40 am bar marks another higher high and confirms our previous trendline.

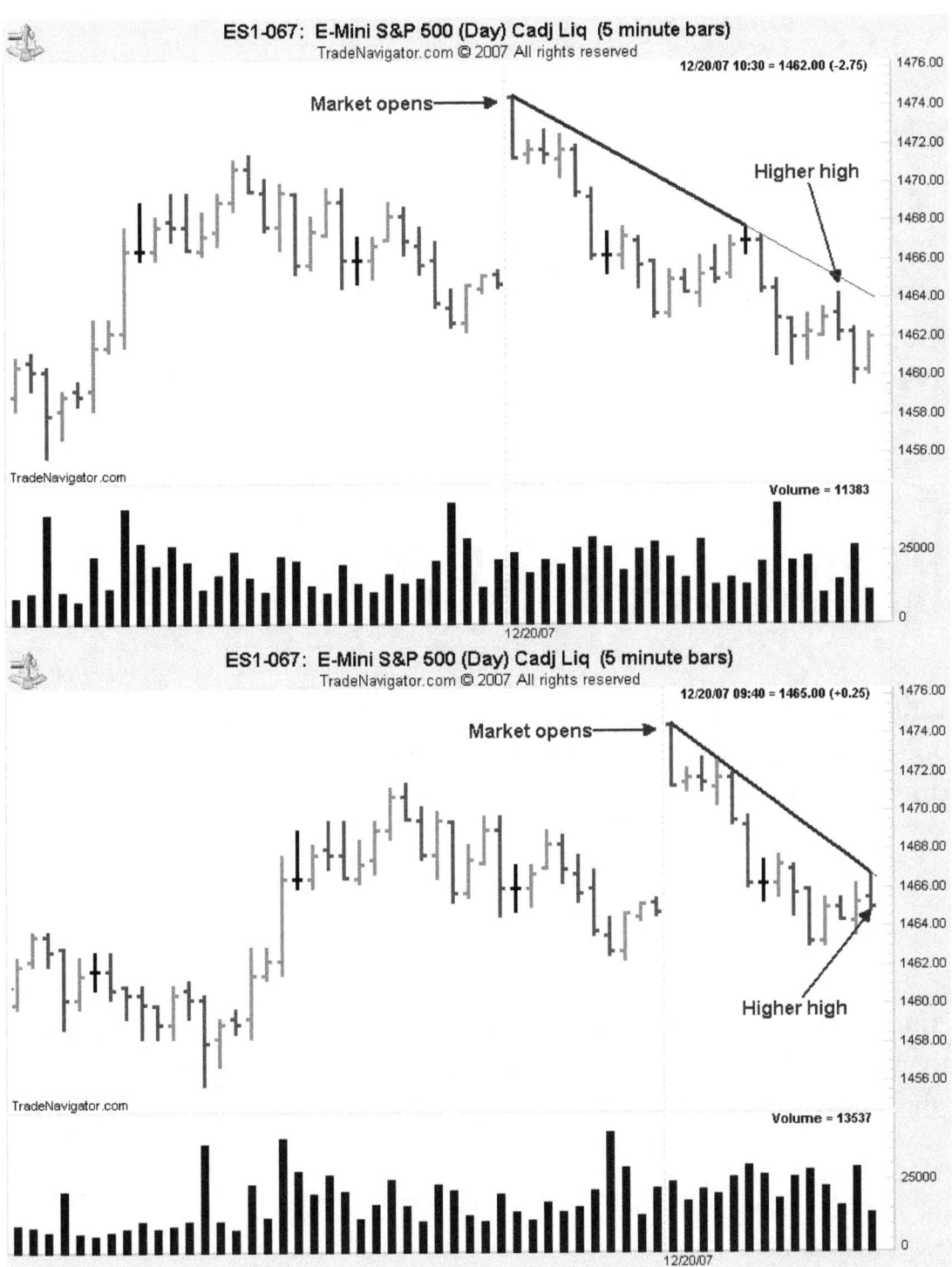

Ten minutes and two bars later, we have another higher high, and we can adjust our line. Note that it's still very close to the previous higher highs, so the adjustment is valid.

The market makes another higher high, but we don't adjust the trendline since it would make the line steeper. See how beautifully our trendline captures It downtrend?

The trend continues, and at 11:15 am, almost three hours after the opening, we can adjust the trendline again. The trendline is still very close to the previous higher highs.

Fifteen minutes later, we get the next higher high, but if we adjust the trendline, it will move too far away from the previous higher highs; the downtrend is broken.

Adjusting the trendline would move it too far away from previous higher highs, and we risk missing a change in the trend.

Trendline Validity

The validity of a trendline is dependent on its duration and the number of times it's been successfully tested.

The longer the trendline has been in effect and the more times it has been successfully tested, the more critical the trendline becomes. Consequently, when a trendline of long duration – which has been successfully tested many times – is violated, an essential reversal of trend is likely to occur.

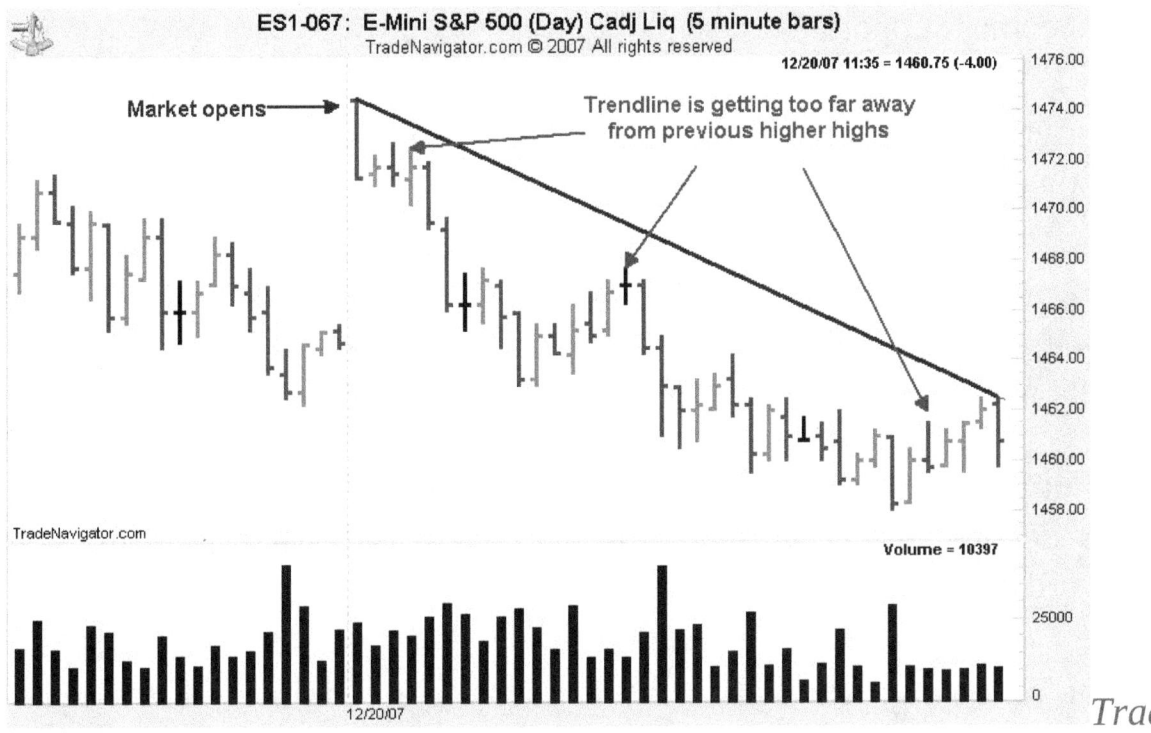

Trading Range

It is a trading pattern that occurs in between an uptrend and a downtrend. It points to equilibrium in supply and demand. Sideways trends follow a horizontal direction, where the price stays relatively constant. Trading patterns are also used to set support and resistance levels, which are very useful for the charts' technical analysis.

Support & Resistance

Support and resistance levels are points where a chart experiences recurring upward or downward pressure. A support level is usually the low point in any chart pattern (hourly, weekly, or annually). In contrast, a resistance level is the high or the peak point of the design.

These points are identified as support and resistance when they show a tendency to reappear. It's best to buy near support or sell near resistance levels that are unlikely to be broken. Once these levels are broken, they invariably reverse their roles. Previous support becomes resistance, and last resistance becomes support.

Support and resistance levels are significant to your trading; you must understand them.

In uptrends, every time the price drops to the uptrend line and then resumes its advance, the trendline has acted as a support to the price uptrend. Help can also be found at prices of previous support or resistance.

In downtrends, every time the price rises to the downtrend line and then resumes its decline, the downtrend line has acted as resistance to market prices' upward movement.

Consider the following: when price action drops to a certain level, the bulls (the buyers) take control and prevent prices from falling lower. Similar to support, a resistance level is a point at which bears (the sellers) take control of costs and prevent them from rising higher.

The price at which a trade takes place is when a bull and bear agree to do business. It represents the consensus of their expectations. The bulls think prices will move higher, and the bears think prices will move lower.

Support levels indicate the price at which most investors believe that prices will move higher. Resistance levels indicate the price at which investors' plurality feels prices will move lower.

The development of support and resistance levels is probably the most noticeable and reoccurring event on price charts.

Example:

As you can see from the following chart, prices have been in a downtrend. On the same bar that broke the downtrend, prices went to the resistance level at 1464.00 and retraced. Ten minutes later, they went two ticks above the resistance level but closed AT the resistance level.

For the next 2 hours and 30 minutes, prices never go above the resistance level of 1464, but they repeatedly test It level, eventually breaking out.

Step 4: Defining Entry Points

As you saw in the previous examples, most of the trading approaches or indicators already provide you with entry rules. When defining entry points, you want to keep it simple and specific. You can't freeze the market. A market is continually moving, and you have to make your trading decisions fast.

Most trading approaches and indicators require a decision at the end of the bar. Even when you're watching 60-minute bars. You've spent the past hour doing nothing except waiting for your signal, now – at the end of the bar – you only have a split second to make your decision.

Use as few entry rules as possible and be as specific as you can. The best trading strategies have entry rules that you can specify in only two lines.

Action Items:

Practice identifying the entry rules of the two approaches you selected. Identify the underlying market condition (trending/ sideways) and apply the strategy you've selected. When should you enter? Only mark the entry points. Don't worry about exit points yet. Continue your trading plan on page 245 and write down your specific entry points under "Entry Signals."

Step 5: Defining Exit Points

This chapter is probably the most important in the entire book. I once heard the saying: "A monkey can enter a trade, but money is made (and lost) when you EXIT it."

It couldn't be more accurate. Most traders are right about the market's direction when they enter a trade, but they end up taking a loss because they fail to capture profits at the right time.

Read this chapter again and again until you understand ALL of the concepts outlined here. Knowing HOW and WHEN to exit a trade will ultimately determine your success or failure as a trader.

There are three different exit rules you should apply:

1.) Stop-loss rules to protect your capital.

2.) Profit-taking exits to realize your gains.

3.) Time-stops to get you out of a trade and free your capital if the market is not moving at all.

Stop loss and profit-taking exit rules can be expressed in four ways:

1.) A fixed dollar amount (e.g. $1,000)

2.) A percentage of the current price (e.g., 1% of the entry price)

3.) A percentage of the volatility (e.g., 50% of the average daily movement)

4.) Based on technical analysis (e.g., support and resistance levels)

In the following, we'll discuss these exit strategies in detail.

Stop Losses

A stop loss is used to limit the potential loss if the trade goes against you. It's the level at which you'll close a transaction on the basis that it has gone too far in the 'wrong' direction and, therefore, negated the reason for you being in that trade.

Always use stop losses!

If you don't apply stop losses in your trading, you won't be trading for long – you'll end up wiping out your trading balance in no time. It can be too easy for a $300 loss to become a $5,000 loss. A good trader will know when to take a small loss and go on to the next trade.

I can't stress this enough: even the most experienced traders have a stop-loss order in the market, whether they're trading forex, futures, options, or even stocks.

Remember that your trading capital is your business – if you burn it, there's no insurance. You're done. Once you've entered a trade, immediately place a stop. It safeguards you from losing your entire account.

Don't Forget Your Stop Losses!

It's essential to ensure that your stop is canceled if you close your positi[on]. [I] mention this because I happen to know a very disciplined trader who al[ways] enters a stop loss and a profit target order once he has established a trade. A years back, this trader suffered several losses over several days. So, naturall[y] was quite happy to see that a transaction finally moved in his direction.

According to his strategy, his stop losses were minimal. His profit target rather large, so if this trade reached the profit target, he would make up for a[l] failures of the past couple of days PLUS bring in a small profit on top of it. it happened: the market continued to move in his favor, and he realized a pro[fit].

He was so happy that he jumped up from his chair, ran into the kitchen, and [told] his wife all about the fantastic trade. FINALLY, he had made some money. [They] enjoyed a happy cup of coffee together, and he couldn't stop talking abou[t his] strategy, the trade, and how it paid off.

And when he returned to his computer an hour later, he found himself in a l[osing] position. He couldn't believe it! How had this happened? After a few minu[tes, it] dawned on him: he had forgotten to cancel his stop loss. While he was celebr[ating] his win, the market retraced, filled his order and continued to go up.

The stop-loss order was a sell order, and now the trader had a short positio[n in a] rising market. All of his profits were gone. The moral of the story:

Make SURE to cancel your orders, or use so-called "bracket orders" or "[one-] cancel-other (OCO) orders" for your profit target and stop loss. Your broke[r can] explain these terms to you in detail.

Regardless of how you approach the decision, the most important thing is to know where you'll cut a losing position BEFORE entering the trade. Set the rules and ALWAYS follow them. With this in mind, let's talk about stop-loss strategies.

Fixed Dollar Amount

Easy, fast, and straightforward. Just specify a dollar amount you're willing to risk, subtract it from your entry price, and place a stop-loss order.

How to Use This Strategy:

Simply subtract the dollar amount you specified from your entry price.

Example:

Let's say you're trading the EUR/USD currency pair. You entered the market at 1.4585, and you want to risk $100. Since one pip (= 0.0001) equals $10, you place your stop loss at ten pips (= 0.0010) below your entry price at 1.4575.

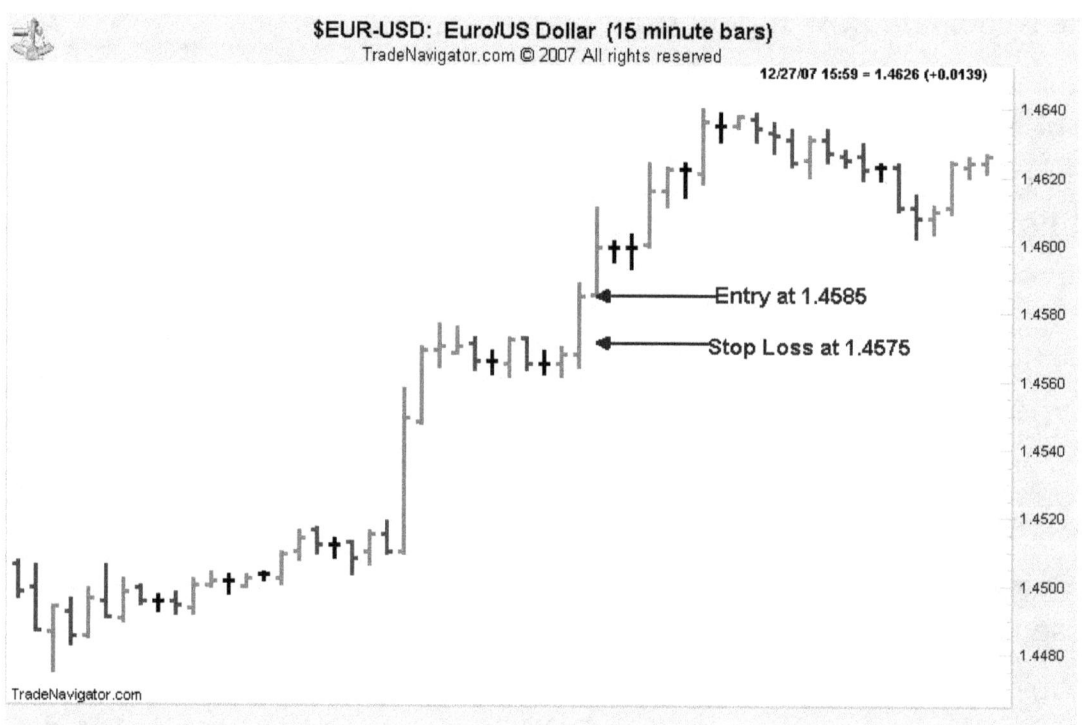

Just as a reminder:

If you're extended security, you'll sell it to close the position. If you're short of security, you'll buy it to close the position. You wouldn't believe how many traders get confused; instead of completing their work, they will add to their job.

It's easy to make mistakes when the market starts moving fast, and you get nervous. Many traders use post-its after they've entered a trade: you stick a 'SELL' post-it on your screen if you went long and a 'BUY' post-it if you went short. This way, you ensure that you'll ALWAYS exit the position as planned.

When to Use This Strategy:

This strategy is perfect for beginners since you don't have to perform complex calculations. You simply add or subtract your stop loss to or from your entry price, and that's it. It works best if you're trading only one stock or one market and if the security doesn't fluctuate too much.

Percentage of the Current Price

How to Use This Strategy:

When applying this stop-loss strategy, simply multiply the entry price by (1 - your stop loss (in percent form)) to get your exit point.

Example:

If you're trading the E-mini NASDAQ, and you've defined a 0.5% stop loss, then you would multiply your entry price of 2151.75 by 0.995 (1 - 0.5%) for an exit point of 2141.

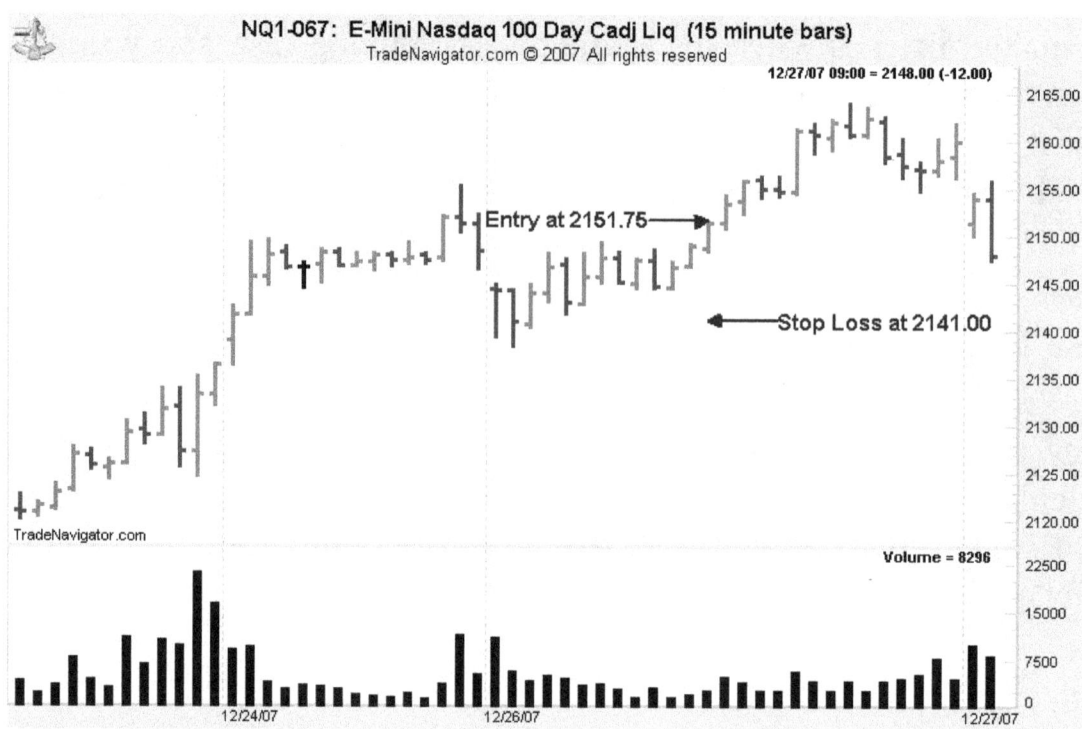

When to Use This Strategy:

You should apply this exit strategy if you're trading multiple markets or different stocks. You'll find a more detailed explanation in the next section: "Profit-Taking Exits."

Percentage of the Volatility

This exit strategy is another way to specify stop losses in volatile markets. The underlying idea is to adjust your stop loss based on the market's volatility: you apply a more considerable stop loss in volatile markets and a smaller stop loss in quiet markets.

How to Use This Strategy:

Using this profit exit strategy requires two steps:

- First, you determine the average volatility of a market.
- Second, multiple this number by the percentage you specified.

Example:

The average daily range in corn is $16. You can use the Average True Range (ATR) function of your charting software to determine this number. Multiply it by the percentage you specified, e.g., 50%, and arrive at a profit target of $8. Then, subtract $8 from your entry point amount.

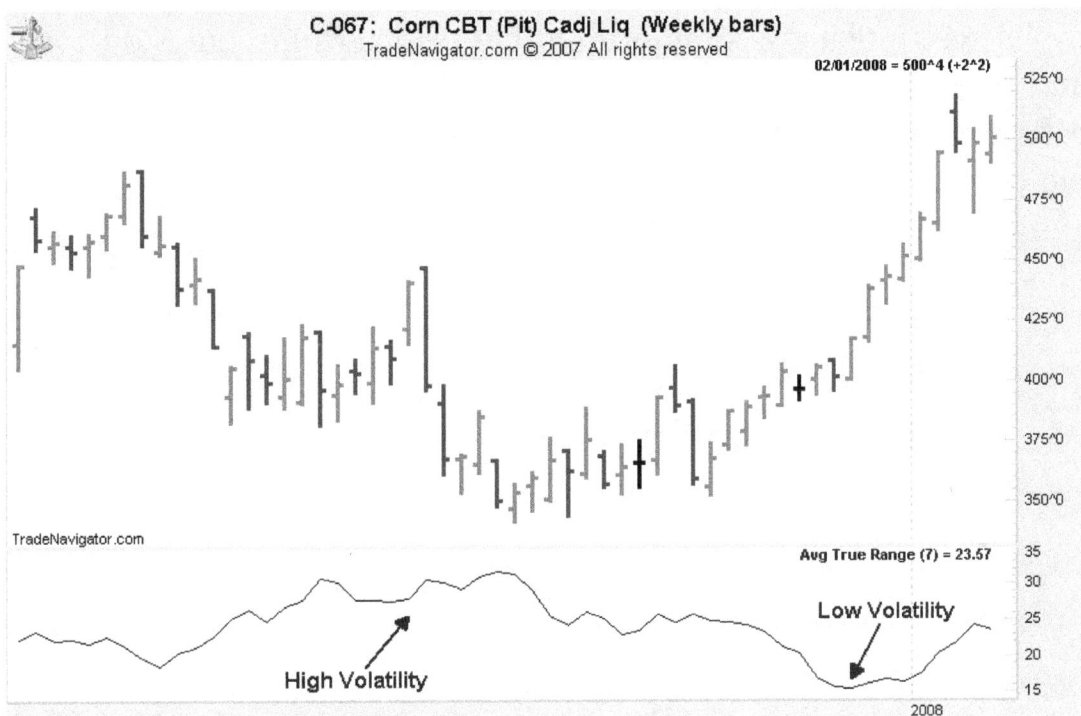

When to Use This Strategy:

This strategy is perfect for markets with significant changes in volatility, as the grain markets. As you can see in the chart below, corn prices are more volatile in the summer months than in the winter.

Many traders like to use major support or resistance points on the chart to determine their exits. Instead of support and resistance levels, you could use Pivot Points, Fibonacci Levels, upper or lower levels of trend channels, or Bollinger Bands, just to name a few.

How to Use This Strategy:

Simply use technical analysis to determine a potential stop loss.

Example:

In this example, we're using a simple trendline to determine our stop loss. The following chart is a 15-minute chart of Apple Computer (AAPL). We wait for the first bar of the day, and as soon as we realize that the stock is moving down over the first 15 minutes, we sell short at $184.80. We draw a trendline from the previous day's high to the high of this morning's bar and set our stop loss at the trendline, at $187.50.

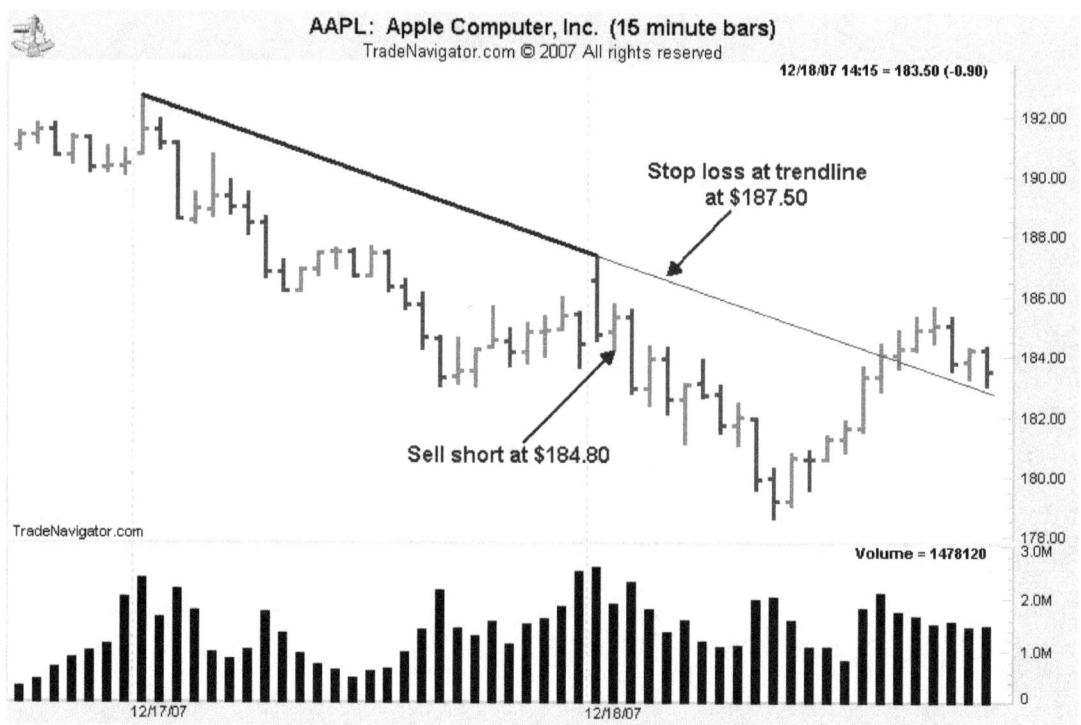

When to Use This Strategy:

This strategy is perfect for traders who use technical analysis for their entry points. If you're using trendlines, indicators, or support and resistance lines, placing your stop at these levels will seem very natural.

Profit-Taking Exits

Once you're in a profitable trade, the next challenge becomes when to take that profit.

The main problem with taking profits is that, by our very nature, we humans (and especially traders) are greedy. After all, we want to make money. A lot of money. And we want to make it fast. "Get rich quick," right?

It is a definite problem, and many traders are way too greedy. They want to get rich on just one trade. And that's when they lose.

Here's the key to trading success: **small profits, consistently**.

Consistency is the key because if your profits are consistent and predictable, then you can simply use leverage to trade size. Therefore you MUST know when to exit with a profit.

Good traders use a stop loss; great traders use a profit target.

Here are some different types of exit strategies for profitable trades.

Fixed Dollar Amount

This is the easiest way to exit a trade. Simply specify a dollar amount that you would be happy with, add it to your entry point, and place a profit target order in the market.

How to Use This Strategy:

Simply add the dollar amount you specified to your entry price.

Example:

Let's say you're trading 100 shares of IBM and enter at $110.13. Your profit target is $100, so you would exit the trade as soon as prices move up $1, to $111.13.

When to Use This Strategy:

This strategy works best if you are just trading one stock or one market, and if the security doesn't fluctuate too much.

Percentage of the Current Price

How to Use This Strategy:

When applying this profit exit strategy, simply multiply the entry price by (1 + your profit target (in percent)) to get your exit point.

Example:

If you're trading IBM, and you've defined a 1% profit target, you would multiply your entry price of $110.13 by 1.01 (1 + 1%) for an exit point of $111.23.

When to Use This Strategy:

You should apply this exit strategy if you are trading multiple markets or different stocks.

The reason is simple: let's say you're trading IBM and Ford. As I write this, IBM is trading at $110.13 and Ford is trading at $6.72. As in the previous example, let's assume that you're trading 100 shares each and you want to make $100 per trade. IBM would only have to move 0.9% to reach your profit target, but Ford shares would have to move almost 15% in order to reach your profit target.

The following charts illustrate how easy it will be for IBM shares to reach the target price, and how difficult it might be for Ford shares to do so.

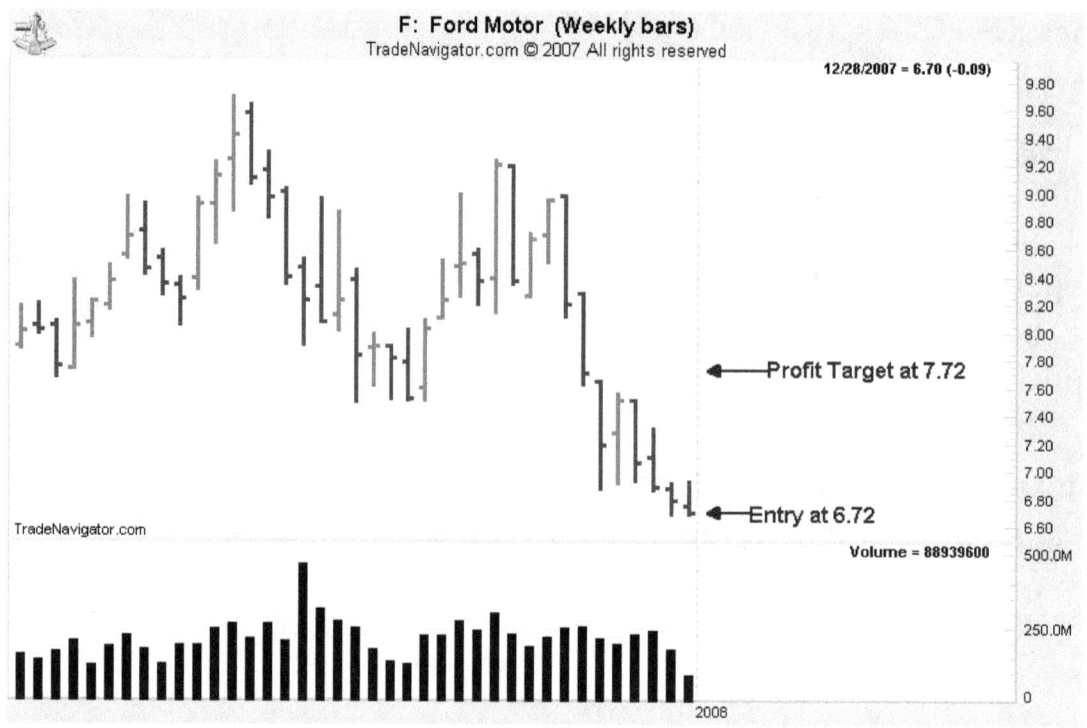

It would make more sense to specify your profit target as a percentage of the price – e.g. 1%. In this case, IBM would have to move $1.1 and Ford only $0.07 to reach the profit target.

The same applies to markets with a high volatility, like gold or energy futures. In the beginning of 2007, gold was trading at $650. In November of 2007, gold was trading 30% higher, at $850. A $20 move in gold would have been 3% in January of 2007, but only 2.3% in November of 2007.

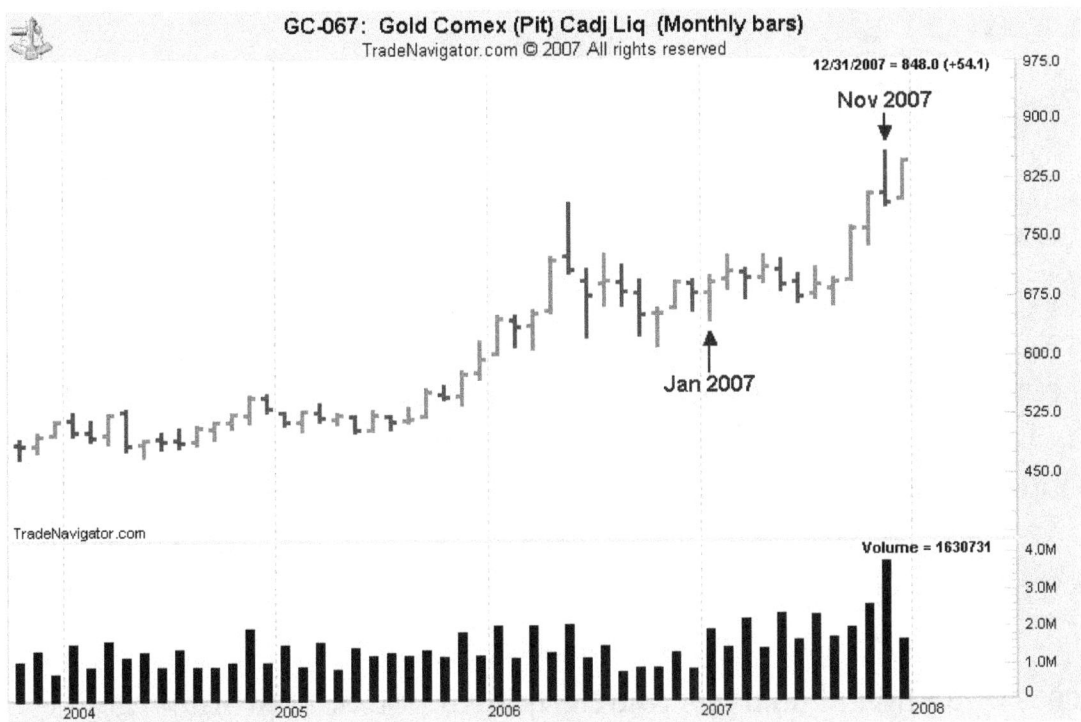

Percentage of the Volatility

This exit strategy is another way to specify profit targets in volatile markets. The underlying idea is to adjust your profit target based on the volatility of the market: you apply a higher profit target in volatile markets and a lower profit target in quiet markets.

How to Use This Strategy:

Using this profit exit strategy requires two steps:

- First, you determine the average volatility of a market.
- Second, multiply this number by the percentage you specified.

Please see the comments in the section on "Stop Losses" as an example.

When to Use This Strategy:

This strategy is perfect for commodity markets with high changes in volatility, like the grain and energy markets.

Using Technical Analysis

Many traders like to use major support or resistance points on the chart to determine their exits. Instead of support and resistance levels, you could use Pivot Points, Fibonacci Levels, upper or lower levels of trend channels, or Bollinger Bands, just to name a few.

How to Use This Strategy:

Use the process of technical analysis to determine a potential profit target.

Example:

In this example, we're using the previous day's high and low as potential profit targets. The following chart is a 15 minute chart of the E-mini S&P. We wait for the first bar of the day, and, as soon as we realize that the market has been moving up in the first 15 minutes, we enter at 1452.

We set our profit target at the previous day's high – 1465.25 – for a total profit of 13.25 points = $662.50. Later that day, we reach our profit target, and we could reverse the position by going short. Now we can use the previous day low as a profit target and realize another profit of 21.75 points = $1,087.50.

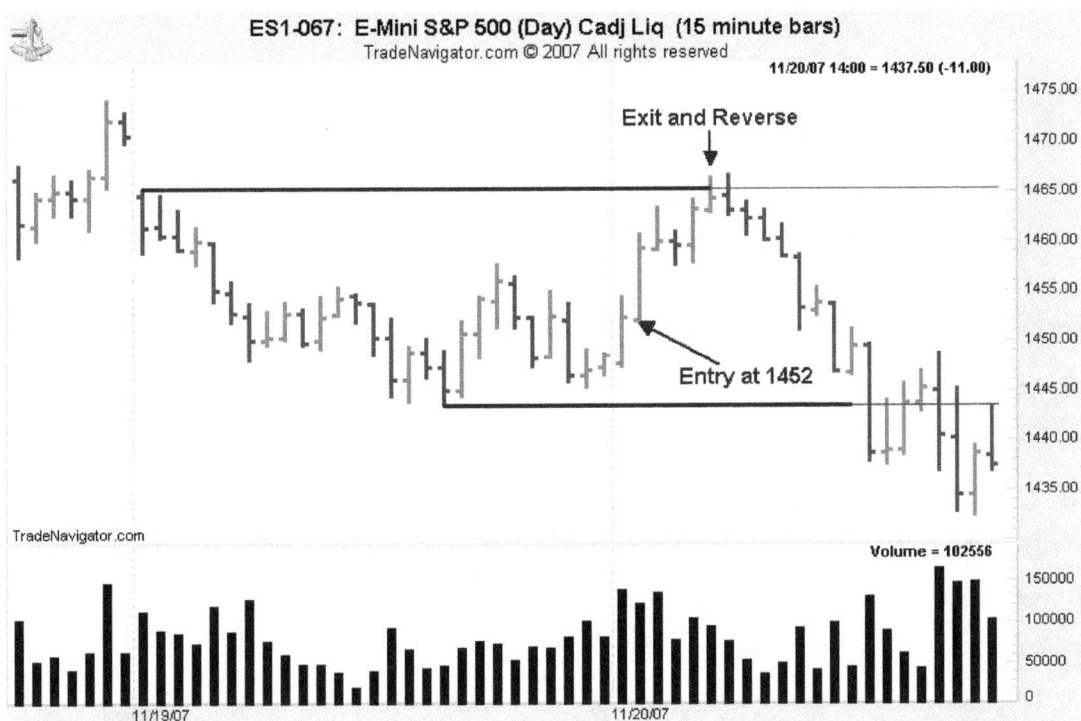

When to Use This Strategy:

This strategy is perfect for markets that are moving sideways between major support and resistance lines.

Trailing Stops

Trailing stops are "hybrid" stops. When entering a position, the trailing stop is typically a stop loss, and as the trade moves in your favor, the trailing stop becomes a profit exit.

The main difference between the exit strategies mentioned previously and trailing stops is that you constantly adjust your stop while you're in a trade. All other exit strategies are "set-it-and-forget-it-strategies," in which you define stop loss and profit exit points the moment you enter the trade, and then leave them alone until you close the trade.

How to Use This Strategy:

This strategy can be used in conjunction with technical analysis by placing the stop at support and resistance lines or – more simply – at the previous bar's high or low. Another popular use of this strategy is placing the stops at trend-following indicators like Moving Averages or Parabolics. Some traders prefer using a fixed dollar amount.

Example 1: Fixed Dollar Amount:

If you were to set a straightforward $300 trailing stop, and the security moved in your favor by $1,000, you could change your stop to only $300 behind the price and lock in $700 of profit.

Example 2: Technical Analysis:

Below is a 60-minute chart of the E-mini S&P. Let's say you went short at 1502. You would place your trailing stop at the high of the current bar at 1504. Once the next bar is completed, you move your stop to the high of this bar to 1502.50. 60 minutes later, you move your stop to 1499, and now your stop loss becomes a profit exit. Whatever happens to the trade now, you'll make at least 3 points (= $150). One hour later, you move your stop to 1494.50.

So, when prices retrace, you're stopped out at 1494.50 for a profit of 7.5 points (= $375).

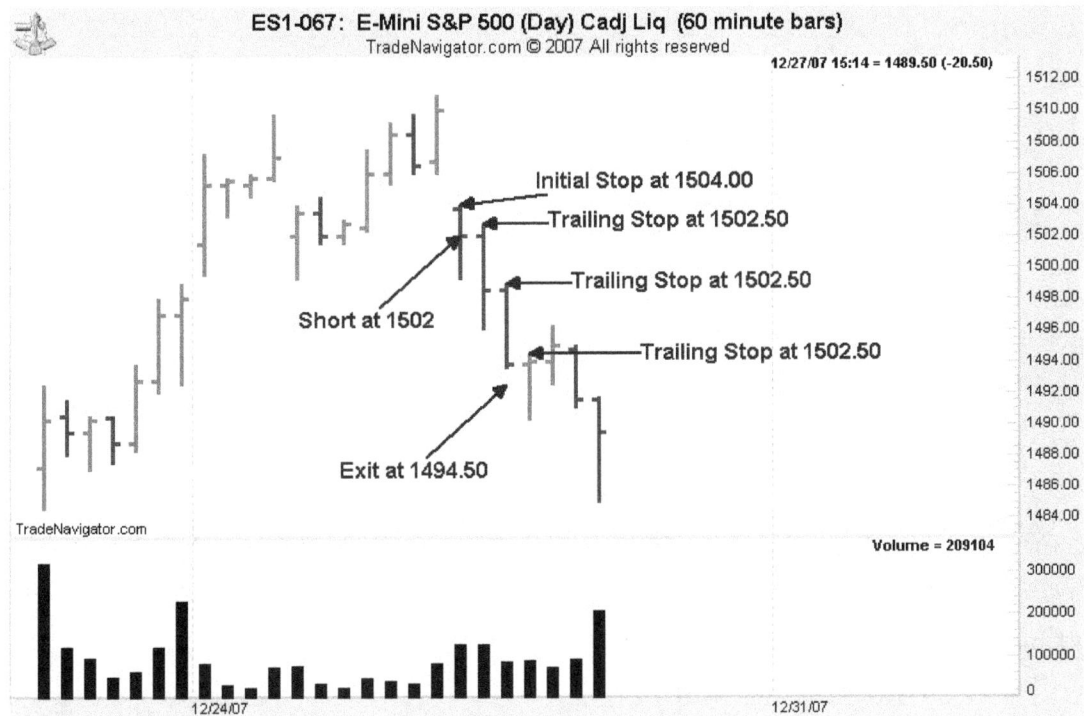

When to Use This Strategy:

This strategy is perfect for trending markets. You should use this strategy to take advantage of longer-lasting trends. Keep in mind that this strategy requires your constant attention, since you MUST move your trailing stops according to your rules.

Taking Partial Profits
Nobody ever lost money taking profits.

You can combine the strategies outlined above for more sophisticated exit strategies. As an example, you could close half of your position once you've achieved a fixed dollar amount in profits, and let the other half continue to trade to the next support or resistance level.

Or you could take 1/3 of your profits at a pre-defined profit target, take another 1/3 at the next support or resistance level, and then apply a trailing stop to the remaining 1/3.

The possibilities are endless. That's why many professional traders focus on perfecting their exit strategy. In contrast, many amateur traders and beginners tend to focus on entry strategies.

Don't make the same mistake. Once you've defined sound entry rules, test different exit strategies to optimize your profits.

Time-Stops

A time-stop gets you out of a trade if it's not moving in any direction. You probably have a good reason for entering a trade. So, immediately after entering, you apply your stop loss and your profit target and wait.
And wait. And wait. And nothing happens.

Time to bail out. If prices do not move at all, get out.

How to Use This Strategy:

Simply specify a "time-out," after which you will exit the market. Then set a timer and exit the trade after the specified time, regardless of whether you reached your stop loss or profit target.

Example:

A good time-stop is three times the timeframe you're using. If you're using 15-minute charts, you might want to abandon the trade if neither your profit nor your stop loss is hit after 45 minutes. If you're using 60 minute charts, get out after 3 hours.

When to Use This Strategy:

Always! Whatever the reason behind your entry signal, you want to see something happen. If nothing happens after a certain amount of time, the underlying assumption of your entry may be wrong. If you stay in the trade, then you're gambling not trading.

As traders, we want to make money fast. The longer you have your money in the market, the longer it's at risk. You can dramatically reduce the risk by applying a time-stop and exiting the market if it doesn't move. Free your capital and take the next trading opportunity. Don't gamble!

Action Items:

> Practice your exit rules: by now you should already be able to spot your entry points. Once you've determined your entry point on a chart, apply your stop loss rule and your profit-taking rule to determine your exit points.

Step 6: Evaluating Your Strategy

Once you've determined which markets you want to trade, selected a timeframe, and defined your entry and exit rules, it's time to test and evaluate your trading strategy.

There are three ways to test your trading strategy:

1.) **Back-Testing**

   Back-testing is a method of testing which will run your strategy against prior time periods. Basically, you're performing a simulation: you use your strategy with relevant past data to test its effectiveness. By using the historical data, you're saving a ton of time; if you tried to test your strategy by applying it to the time periods yet to come, it might take you years.

   Back-testing is used for a variety of strategies, including those based on technical analysis. The effectiveness of back-testing relies on the theory that what has happened in the past WILL happen again in the future. Also, keep in mind that your back-testing results are quite dependent on the moves that occurred in the tested time period. It's important to remember that this increases the potential of risk for your strategy.

2.) **The Monte-Carlo Simulation**

   The Monte-Carlo Simulation is a problem-solving technique used to approximate the probability of certain outcomes by running multiple trial runs – called simulations – using random variables. It is a way to account for the randomness in a trading parameter – typically, the sequence of trades. In Monte Carlo simulations, the basic idea is to take a sequence of trades generated by a trading system, randomize the order of trades, and calculate the rate of return and the maximum drawdown, assuming that x% of the account is risked on each trade.

The process is repeated several hundred times, each time using a different random sequence of the same trades. You can then pose a question such as "If 5% of the account is risked on each trade, what is the probability that the maximum drawdown will be less than 25%?" If 1,000 random sequences of trades are simulated with 5% risk, for example, and 940 of them have a maximum drawdown of less than 25%, then you could say the probability of achieving a maximum drawdown of less than 25% is 94% (940/1,000).

Keep in mind that the data used in Monte Carlo Simulations is still historical data; therefore, one could say that this simulation is a more sophisticated way of back-testing.

3.) **Paper Trading**

Paper trading is a method of "risk-free" trading. Basically, you set up a dummy account, through which you can test your trading strategy with paper money. There are two methods to this: you can either pretend to buy and sell stocks, bonds, commodities, etc., and keep track of your profits and losses on paper, or you can open an account online, usually through your broker (and usually for free).

This is a fantastic way for new traders to kill a whole tree full of birds with one stone. First off, you'll learn the tricks of the trade without putting your own money at risk. Second, you'll be able to gain some much-needed confidence when it comes to maneuvering in the markets. And third, you'll be able to test out your trading strategy in real-time simulation.

This is probably the best way to test a trading strategy, since it doesn't rely on historical data. On the other hand, it's the most time-consuming strategy, since it might take weeks or months until you have enough data for a statistically relevant performance report.

How long should you back-test a trading strategy?

The more trades you use in your back-testing, the higher the probability that your trading strategy will succeed in the future. Look at the following table:

Number of Trades	50	100	200	300	500
<>Margin of Error	14%	10%	7%	6%	4%

More trades mean a smaller margin of error, resulting in a higher predictability of future performance.

Somebody with a Ph.D. in statistics once told me that you need at least 40 trades in order to produce statistically relevant results.

So, the question "How <u>long</u> should you test your trading strategy?" depends on the trade frequency.

How many trades per day does your trading strategy generate? Suppose your method generates three transactions per day (i.e., 15 trades per week). In that case, you might get decent results after three weeks of testing. But suppose your trading strategy generates only three trades per month (i.e., 36 transactions per year). In that case, you should test your system for at least one year to receive reliable data results.

When testing a strategy, keep in mind that markets change.

Let me use the E-mini S&P as an example. In 2000, the average daily range was 100-150 ticks per day; in 2004, it was only 40-60 ticks per day.

Suppose you back-test any trend-following day trading system in the E-mini S&P. In that case, and you'll see that it worked perfectly until 2002. Then, suddenly, it fell apart. It seems that there were no more intraday trends. That's not surprising as the daily range of the E-mini S&P decreased by more than 50%.

What happened?

There are a couple of plausible explanations. The best and most important one is the introduction of the Pattern Day Trading Rule in August and September of 2001 by the NYSE and NASD. Suppose a trader executes four or more day trades within a five-business-day period. In that case, he must maintain minimum equity of $25,000 in his margin account at all times. Because of this rule, traders stopped day trading equities and started trading the E-mini S&P futures instead.

Look at this graph showing the sudden increase in volume in the E-mini S&P at the beginning of 2001.

Many of these stock day traders used methods to scalp the market for a few pennies. Using the E-mini S&P, they suddenly had much higher leverage and paid fewer commissions, and their plans were extremely profitable.

Unfortunately, these scalping methods kill an intraday trend almost instantly, making almost every trend-following approach fail.

Another reason for the dramatic change of the market was introducing the automated strategy execution in TradeStation. In 2002, the TradeStation customers who were using this feature increased by 268%. Overbought/oversold strategies became very popular, and when the market attempted to trend, these strategies immediately established a contrary position.

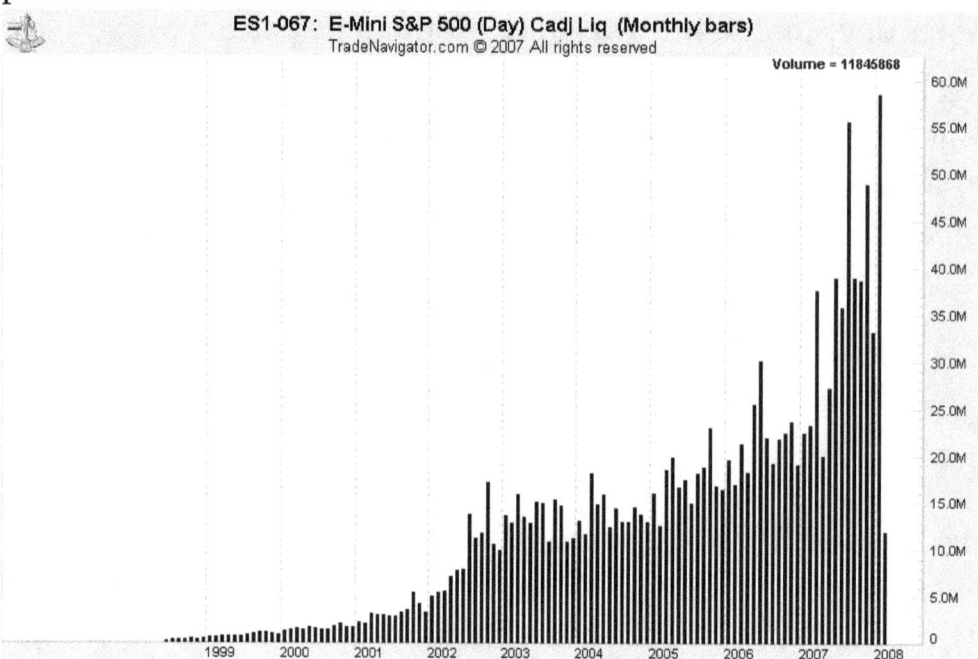

Conclusion

When back-testing, there are things you need to be aware of. It's not enough to just run a strategy on as much data as possible; it's essential to know the underlying market conditions.

As outlined in previous chapters: in non-trending markets, you need to use trend-fading systems; and, in trending markets, you should use trend following methods.

That's when clever back-testing helps you. If your back-testing tells you that a trend-following method worked in 2000-2002, but doesn't work in 2003 and 2004, then you should not use this strategy right now. And vice versa: when you see that a trend-fading method produced nice profits in 2003, 2004, and 2005, then trade it.

How to Read and Understand a Performance Report

While testing your trading strategy, you should keep detailed records of the wins and losses to produce a performance report. Many software packages can help you with that, but a simple excel sheet will do the trick just as well.

Get in contact with us here at Rockwell Trading®. We can send you an excel sheet that will automatically produce a performance report for you after you've entered several trades.

Here's an example of a performance report:

Performance Report for Florian

Number of Trades		34
Total Profit	$	4,300.00
Avg. Profit per Trade	$	126.47
Winning Percentage		73.53%
Avg Winning Trade	$	206.00
Avg. Losing Trade	$	(94.44)
Profit Factor ($Wins/$Loss)		6.06
Max Drawdown	$	(200.00)

Total (Net) Profit

The first figure to look for is the total, or net, profit. You want your system to generate profits, but don't be frustrated when, during the development stage, your trading system shows a loss; try to reverse your entry signals.

You might have heard that trading is a zero-sum game. If you want to buy something (e.g., a specific stock or futures contract), somebody else needs to sell it to you. And, you can only sell a position if somebody else is willing to buy from you at the price you're asking.

It means that if you lose money on a trade, then the person who took the other side of the transaction is MAKING money. And vice versa: if you're making money on an exchange, then the other trader is losing money. In the markets, money is not "generated." It just changes hands.

So, if you're going long at a certain price level, and you lose, then try to go short instead. Many times this is the easiest way to turn a losing system into a winning one.

Average Profit per Trade

The next figure you want to look at is the average profit per trade. Make sure this number is more significant than slippage and commissions and that it makes your trading worthwhile. Trading is all about risk and reward, and you want to make sure you get decent compensation for your trouble.

Winning Percentage

Many profitable trading systems achieve a nice net profit with a relatively small winning percentage, sometimes even below 30%. These systems follow the principle: "Cut your losses short and let your profits run." However, YOU need to decide whether you can stand seven losers and only three winners in 10 trades. If you want to be "right" most of the time, you should pick a high winning percentage system.

Understanding Winning Percentage

Let's say you purchased or developed a system that has a winning percentage of 70%.

What exactly does that mean?

It means that the probability of having a winning trade is 70%. I.e., it is more likely that the transaction you are currently in turns out to be a winner rather than a loser.

Does that mean that when you trade ten times, you will have seven winners?

No!

It means that if you trade long enough (i.e., at least 40 trades), then you will have more winners than losers. But it doesn't guarantee that after three losers in a row, you'll have a winner.

Example:

If you toss a coin, then you have two possible outcomes: heads or tails. The probability for each is 50% – i.e., when you throw the cash four times, you should get two heads and two tails.

But what if you tossed the coin three times and you got heads three times?

What is the probability of heads on the fourth coin toss?

50% or less?

If you answered 'less,' then you fell for a common misconception. The probability of getting heads again is still 50%. No more and no less.

But many traders think that the probability of tails is higher now because the three previous coin tosses resulted in heads. Some traders might even increase their bet because they are convinced that now "tails is overdue." Statistically, this assumption is nonsense; it's a dangerous – and many times costly – misconception.

> Let's get back to our trading example: if you have a winning percentage of 70%, and you had nine losers in a row, what's the probability of having a winner now? It's still 70% (and therefore, there's always a 30% chance of a loser).

Average Winning Trade and Average Losing Trade

The average winning trade should be more significant than the average losing trade. If you can keep your wins larger than your losses, you'll make money even if you just have a 50% winning percentage. And every trader should be able to achieve that. If you can't, reverse your entry signals as described previously.

Profit Factor

Take a look at the Profit Factor (Gross Profit / Gross Loss). It will tell you how many dollars you're likely to win for every dollar you lose. The higher the profit factor, the better the system. A system should have a profit factor of 1.5 or more, but watch out when you see profit factors above 3.0 because it might be that the system is over-optimized.

Maximum Drawdown

The maximum drawdown is the lowest point your account reaches between peaks.

Let me explain:

Imagine that you start your trading account with $10,000, and, after a few trades, you lose $2,000. Your drawdown would be 20%.

Now, let's say you make more trades and gain $4,000, which brings you to

$12,000 ($8,000 + $4,000 = $12,000). And after this, on the next trade, you lose $2,000. Your drawdown would be 16.7% ($12,000 - $2,000). The $12,000 was your equity peak; that was the highest point in the period we looked at.

If you started your account with $10,000 and the lowest amount you had in your account over six months was $5,000, then you had a 50% drawdown.

You would need to make $5,000 from the lowest point to recoup your losses. Even though you lost 50% from your high of $10,000, you would need to make 100% on the $5,000 to get back to your original amount.

Measuring Drawdown Recovery:

Drawdown recovery can confuse many traders. If a trader loses 20% of his account, he thinks he needs to make 20% to get back to even.

It isn't true. If you started with $10,000 and lost $2,000 (20%), you would need to make 25% to get back to even. The difference between $8,000 and $10,000 is $2,000. If you calculate the $2,000 as a percentage of $8,000 (not the original $10,000), it works out to 25%.

A famous trader once said: "If you want your system to double or triple your account, you should expect a drawdown of up to 30% on your way to trading riches." Not every trader can stand a 30% drawdown.

Look at the maximum drawdown that your strategy has produced so far, and double it. If you can stand this drawdown, then you've found the right strategy.

Why double it? Remember: your worst drawdown is always ahead of you. It's best to plan for it now.

Conclusion

The above examples provide you with some guidelines. Still, it's up to you to decide whether the numbers in the strategy's performance report work for you or don't.

Ultimately, YOU'RE the one trading the strategy, and YOU'RE the one who has to feel comfortable with the expected results of your strategy.

Action Items:

    Start back-testing your trading plan on at least 40 trades. The more transactions, the better. You can download an excel sheet to record your transactions from our website:

    www.thecompleteguidetodaytrading.com

    Analyze the performance report and decide if YOU feel comfortable with the statistics.

Step 7: Improving Your Strategy

There is a difference between "improving" and "curve-fitting" a system. You can improve your technique by testing different exit methods. If you're using a fixed stop, try a trailing finish instead. Add a time-stop and re-evaluate the results.

Don't look only at the net profit; also look at the profit factor, the average profit per trade, and the maximum drawdown. You'll often see that the net profit slightly decreases when you add different stops, but the other figures might improve dramatically.

Don't fall into the trap of over-optimizing: you can eliminate almost all losers by adding enough rules, but your resulting strategy will be almost worthless.

Example:

If you see that you have more losers on Tuesdays than on the other weekdays, you might be tempted to add a "filter" that prevents your system from entering trades on Tuesdays.

Next, you find that you have much worse results in January than in other months, so you add a filter that enters trades only between February and December.

You add more and more filters to avoid losses, and eventually, you end up with a trading rule like this, which I just saw recently:

> *IF FVE > -1 And Regression Slope (Close , 35) / Close.35 * 100*
> *> -.35 And Regression Slope (Close , 35) / Close.35 ***
> *100 < .4 And Regression Slope (Close , 70) / Close.70 * 100*
> *> -.4 And Regression Slope (Close , 70) / Close.70 * 100 <*
> *.4 And Regression Slope (Close , 170) / Close.170 * 100 > .2 And*

> *MACD Diff (Close , 12 , 26 , 9) > -.003 And Not Tuesday And Not Day Of Month = 12 and not Month = August and Time > 9:30 ...*

Though you've eliminated all possibilities of losing (in the past), and this trading system is now producing fantastic profits in your testing, it's doubtful that it will continue to do so when it hits reality.

Determine the "Best" Parameter Without Curve-Fitting a Strategy

The underlying strategy in this example is a simple breakout strategy.
The strategy contains a parameter called **TF_Param**.

I'll explain how we optimized the parameter and why we selected 0.3 as the parameter's current value. I used **Genesis Financial Trade Navigator** (www.genesisft.com) to produce the test results and the following graphics.

First, I run the optimization and look at the net profit, since that's one of the most important figures:

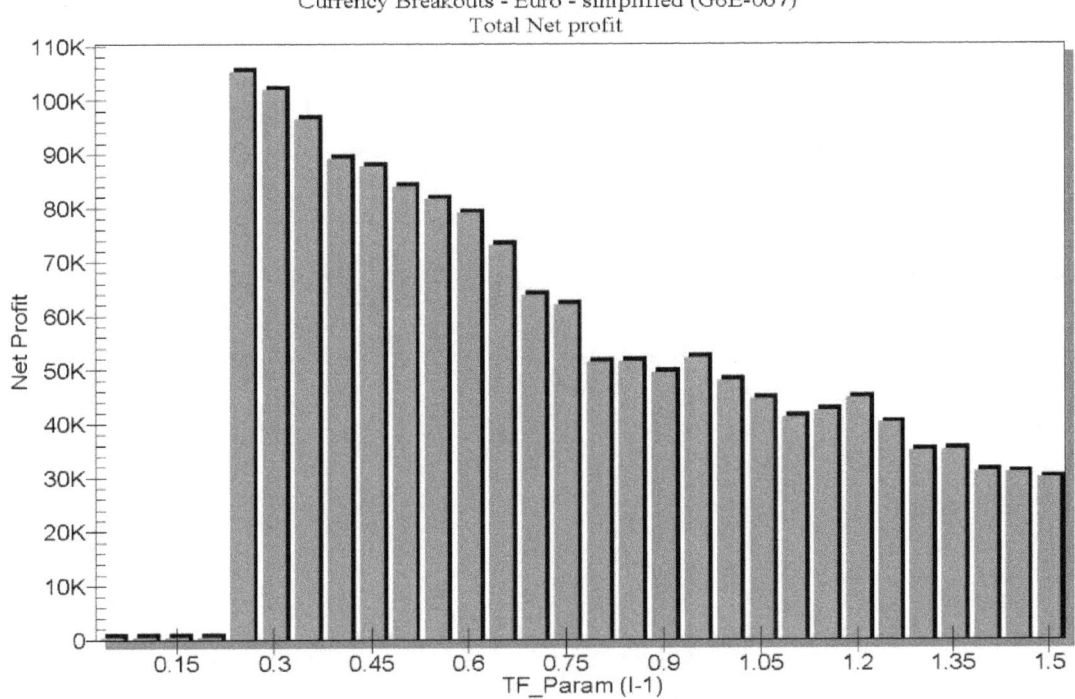

As you can see, a parameter between 0.25 and 0.7 produces robust results. Next, I am looking at the max drawdown.

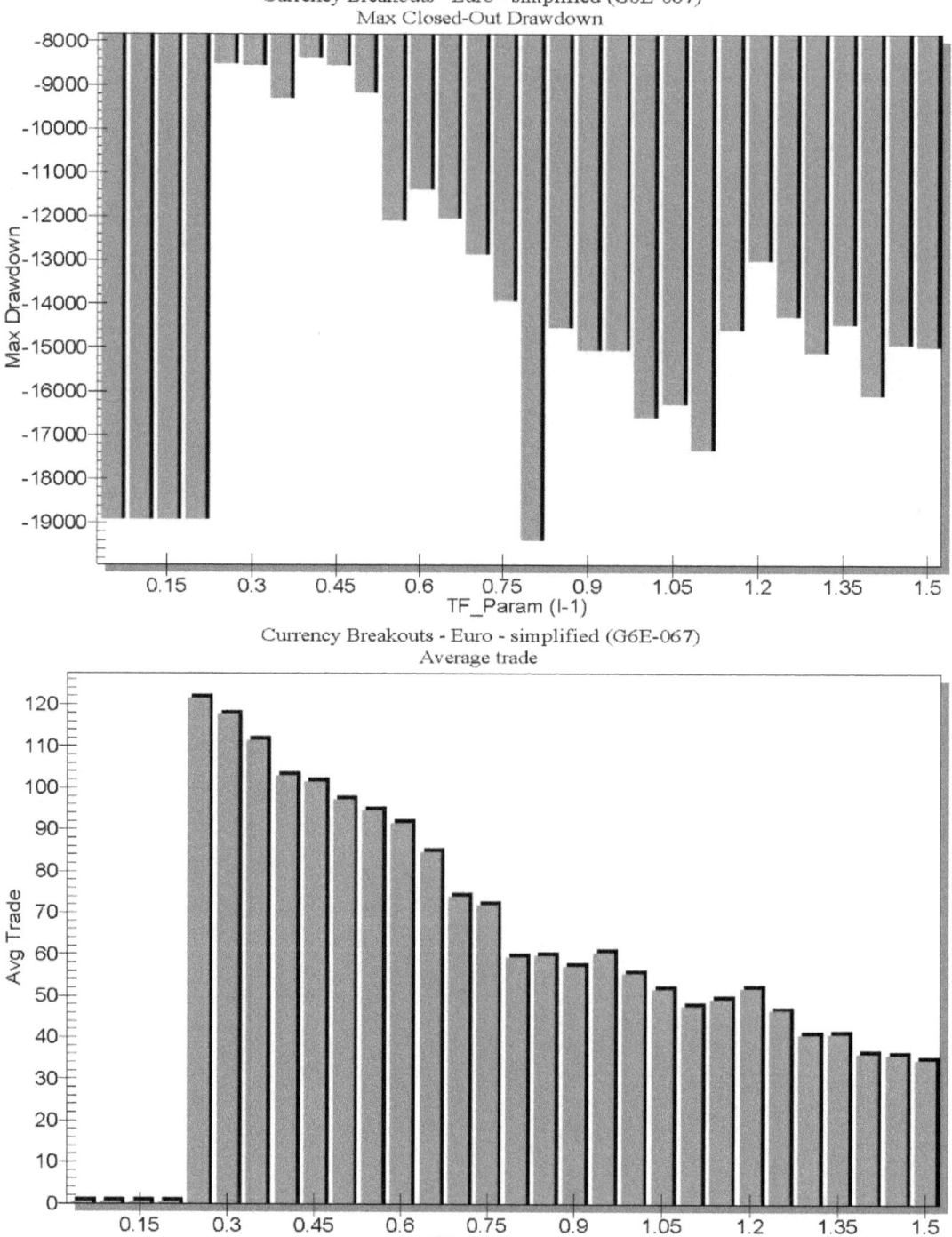

Any parameter between 0.25 and 0.5 produces a relatively low drawdown, so using the combined information, I would pick a TF_Param between 0.25 and 0.5.

Now, I'm looking at the average profit per trade:

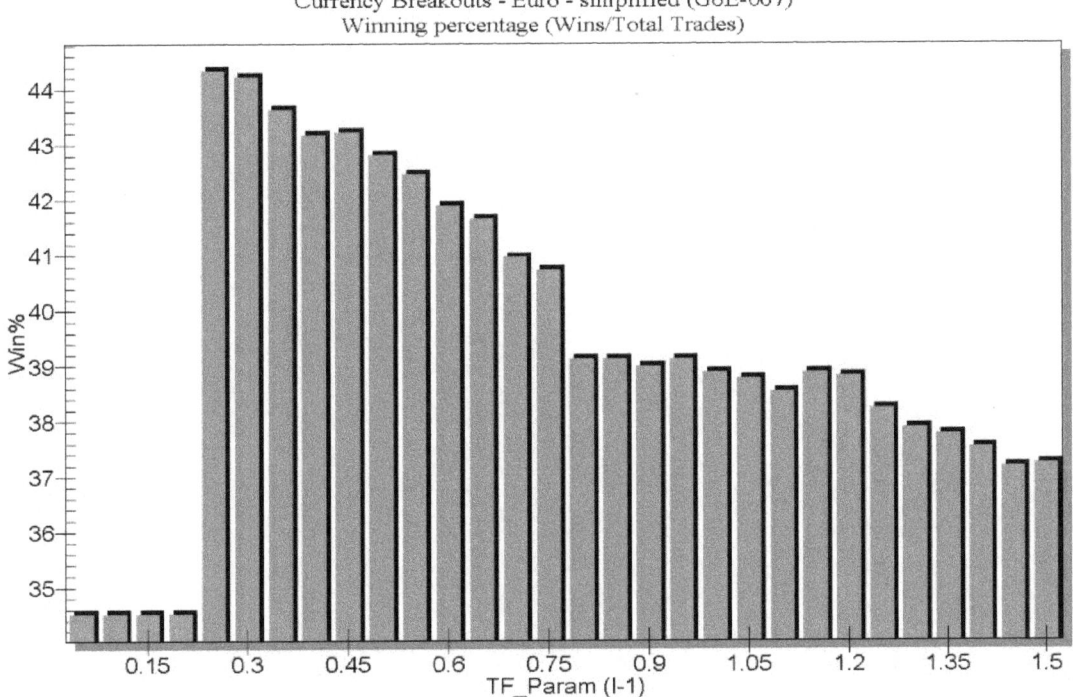

A parameter between 0.25 and 0.7 produces a decent average profit per trade, so the current selection of TF_Param between 0.25 and 0.5 is still the right choice.

Now, I'm looking at the winning percentage. The higher, the better:

Again a value of 0.25 to 0.7 for the variable TF_Param produces the best results. We leave our range for TF_Param between 0.25 and 0.5

As the last test, we look at the number of trades. Again, the higher, the better.

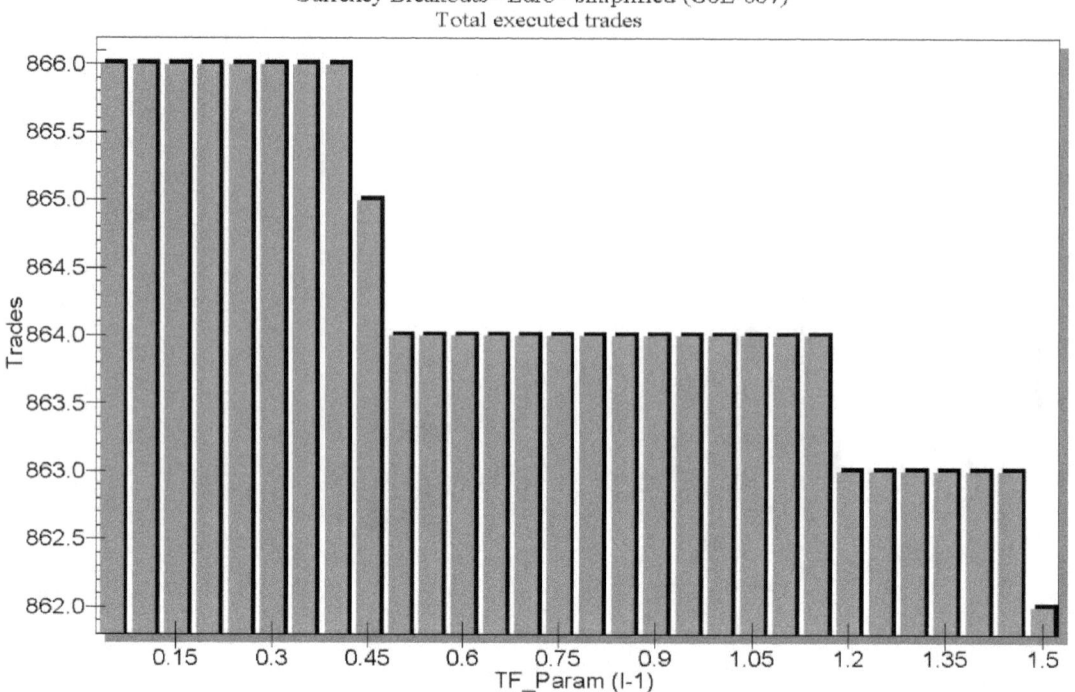

No surprises here: the lower the parameter, the more trades we get. A parameter value below 0.45 leads to the highest amount of transactions.

Conclusion

By combining all the previous findings, we see that a TF_Param between 0.25 and 0.4 produces the best results.

That's why 0.3 is the right choice. Even if the market changes slightly, the system would still produce excellent results.

Action Items:

>Try to improve your trading strategy by varying the parameters. As an example: if you used 14 bars in the RSI, try 10, 12, 14, 16, 18, and 20 bars.

Try to improve your strategy by modifying the stops.

Example: use a volatility stop instead of a fixed stop loss.

Do the same with your profit targets. I know that this is time-consuming, but the good news is, once it's done correctly, you won't have to do it again for a very long time. I have been using the same trading strategy for four years now.

****

Chapter 11

The 10 Power Principles – Making Sure That Your Trading Plan Works

Having a trading plan is like having a solid blueprint for building your home or map when traveling to a new location. You already know that a professional trader won't survive in the markets without a good trading plan.

In the previous step, you learned:

- How to define your financial and trading goals.
- How to select the right market for your trading goals.
- What timeframe you should trade-in.
- Different trading styles and how to find the right one for you.
- How to create a basic trading plan.

Now that you've defined your goals and created your trading plan, you need to make sure it works. Thus far, everything might look great, but how can you be sure that the system works when you start trading it with real money?

Evaluating a trading strategy is easier than you think. In this chapter, you'll **find 10 Principles of Successful Trading Strategies** that we've developed and refined over the last couple of years.

You should use these Power Principles to evaluate your trading strategy, whether you developed it on your own or think about purchasing one. By checking an approach against these principles, you can dramatically increase your chances of success.

Principle #1: Use Few Rules – Make It Easy to Understand
It may surprise you that the best trading systems have less than ten rules. The

more restrictions you have, the more likely it that you've "curve-fitted" your trading strategy to past data, and such an over-optimized system is improbable to produce profits in real markets.

Your rules must be easy to understand and execute. The markets can behave very wildly and move very fast. You won't have time to calculate complicated formulas to make a trading decision. Think about successful floor traders: the only tool they use is a calculator. They make thousands of dollars every day.

Example:

Take a look at the trading approaches presented in the section "Popular Trading Approaches." The easy rules are: buy when the RSI drops below a reading of 20, or sell when prices move above the upper Bollinger Band.

Avoid a trading strategy that has an entry rule like this:

> *But when the RSI is below 20, and the ADX is between 7 and 12, and the 7-bar moving average is pointing up more than 45 degrees, and there is a convergence between the price bars and the MACD, and, and, and...*

Do you think that you could follow this strategy while you're watching the markets LIVE?

Principle #2: Trade Electronic and Liquid Markets

I strongly recommend that you trade electronic markets because commissions are lower and you receive instant fills. You need to know as fast as possible if your order was filled and at what price because you plan your exit based on this information.

You should never place an exit order before you know that your entry order is filled. When you trade open outcry markets (non-electronic), you might have to wait a while before you receive your fill. By that time, the market might have already turned, and your profitable trade has turned into a loss!

When trading electronic markets, you receive your fills in less than one second and immediately place your exit orders. Trading liquid markets mean you can avoid slippage, which will save you hundreds or even thousands of dollars.

Fortunately, more and more markets are now traded electronically. The recent addition of the grain futures markets in the summer of 2006 was a huge success. In January of 2007, the volume traded in the electronic contracts surpassed the volume traded in the pit markets. In December of 2007, the pit-traded corn contract sold with 621,800 deals. The electronic corn contract had a trading volume of 2,444,400 contracts.

Most futures markets, all forex currency pairs, and the major U.S. stock markets are trading electronically.

So why would you even want to trade Pork Bellies or Lumber?

Principle #3: Have Realistic Expectations

Losses are part of our business. A trading system that doesn't have losses is "too good to be true." Recently, I ran into a trading system with a whopping winning percentage of 91% and a drawdown of less than $500.
WOW!

When I looked at the details, though, it turned out that the system was only tested on 87 trades, and – of course – it was curve-fitted. If you run across a trading system with numbers too good to be true, then it's probably precisely THAT: too good to be true.

Usually, you can expect the following from a robust trading system:

1.) A winning percentage of 60-80%
2.) A profit factor of 1.3-2.5
3.) A maximum drawdown of 10-20% of the yearly profit

Use these numbers as a rough guideline, and you'll quickly identify curve fitted systems.

Principle #4: Maintain a Healthy Balance Between Risk and Reward

Let me give you an example: if you go to a casino and bet everything you have on "red," you have a 49% chance of doubling your money and a 51% chance of losing everything. The same applies to trading: you can make a lot of money if you're risking a lot, but if you do, the risk of ruin is also high. You need to find a healthy balance between risk and reward.

Make sure your trading strategy uses small stop losses and that your profit targets are more significant than your stop losses.

Stay away from strategies with a small profit target of only $100 and a stop loss of $2,000. Sure, the winning percentage will be fantastic, but 2-3 losses in a row can wipe out your trading account.

The perfect balance between risk and reward is 1:1.5 or more – i.e., for every dollar you risk, you should be able to make at least $1.50.

In other words, if you apply a stop loss of $100, your profit target should be at least $150.

Principle #5: Find a System That Produces at Least Five Trades per Week

The higher your trading frequency, the smaller your chances of having a losing month. If you have a trading strategy with a winning percentage of 70% but only produces one trade per month, then one loser is enough to have a losing month. In this example, you could have several losing months in a row before you finally start making profits.

In the meantime, how do you pay your bills?

If your trading strategy produces five trades per week, you have on average 20 transactions per month. If you have a winning percentage of 70%, your chances of winning a month are incredibly high.

And that's the goal of all traders: having as many winning months as possible!

Principle #6: Start Small – Grow Big

Your trading system should allow you to start small and grow big. A sound trading system will enable you to create one or two contracts, increasing your position as your trading account grows.

It contrasts with many "martingale" trading systems, which require increasing position sizes when you are losing streak.

Your First Trade	$100	1 contract or 100 shares
Second Trade	$200	2 contracts or 200 shares
Third Trade	$400	4 contracts or 400 shares
Fourth Trade	$800	8 contracts or 800 shares
Fifth Trade	$1,600	16 contracts or 1,600 shares
Sixth Trade	$3,200	32 contracts or 3,200 shares
Seventh		

You've probably heard about this strategy: Double your contracts every time you lose, and one winner will win back all the money you previously lost.

Trade	$6,400	64 contracts or 6,400 shares
Eighth Trade	$12,800	128 contracts or 12,800 shares
Ninth Trade	$25,600	256 contracts or 25,600 shares
Tenth Trade	$51,200	512 contracts or 51,200 shares
Your Total Loss	**$102,300**	**1,024 contracts or 102,400 shares**

Let's take a look at the following table. It assumes that you are risking $100 per trade and then doubling up after each losing trade.

As you can see from the chart, the losses are not the problem; the main problem is the number of contracts or shares you're trading.

It's not unusual to have 4-5 losing trades in a row, and this strategy would already require you to trade 16 contracts, or 1,600 shares, of stock after just four losses! If you're changing the E-mini S&P, you would need an account size of at least $63,200, only to meet the margin requirements. If we assume that you're trading stocks around $100 (e.g., IBM or Apple), you would need $160,000 in your account.

Now, you may ask how likely this type of situation is. The answer: very reasonable. That was the entire point of the previous few pages. Just think back to the example with the coins: an atypical negative trading run CAN and WILL happen.

It is why I do not recommend doubling up after each loss. If we trade in a disciplined, systematic manner, then when our atypical run DOES occur, we will still be in the game at the end of it.

Regardless of the strategy or method you use to trade, there will be occasions when you have losses or even a string of losses. When these occur, it's essential to have faith in your trading plan; don't try to double up your trades to "catch up" on your wins.

I want to make here that every trading system you find will go through times when it has more losses than wins.

It is to be expected, and it's where effective money management comes into play.

Principle #7: Automate Your Exits

Emotions and human errors are the most common mistakes that traders make. You have to avoid these mistakes by any means necessary, especially when the market moves fast. You might experience panic and indecision, but if you give in to those emotions, you'll suffer a much more significant loss than you had initially planned for.

Your exit points should be easy to determine. The best solution for your exit points is the use of "bracket orders." Most trading platforms offer bracket orders, which allow you to attach a profit target and a stop loss to your entry.

This way, you can put your trade on autopilot, and the trading system will close your position at the specified levels.

Of course, this assumes that you have easy exit rules. A stop loss of $100, or 1%, of the entry price, can easily be specified in today's trading platforms.

Exit rules like "2/3 of the true average range of the past five trading days" are more complex to automate. In the beginning, you should keep your trading as simple as possible.

If you can't make money with simple entry and exit points, you won't make money with more complex trading rules. Think about driving a car: if you can't go a Ford, you definitely won't be able to drive a Ferrari.

Principle #8: Have a High Percentage of Winning Trades

Your trading strategy should produce more winners than 50%. There's no doubt that trading strategies with smaller winning percentages can be profitable, too, but the psychological pressure is enormous.

Taking seven losers out of 10 trades and not doubting that system takes a great deal of discipline, and many traders can't stand the pressure. After the sixth loser, they'll start "improving" the strategy or stop trading it altogether.

It's beneficial for beginning or novice traders to gain confidence in their trading. If your strategy gives you a high winning percentage, let's say more than 65%, your confidence will be on the rise.

Principle #9: Test Your Strategy on at Least 200 Trades

The more trades you use in your back-testing (without curve-fitting), the higher the probability that your trading strategy will succeed in the future. Look at the following table:

Number of Trades	50	100	200	300	500
<>Margin of Error	14%	10%	7%	6%	4%

The more trades you have in your back-testing, the smaller the margin of error, and the higher the probability of producing profits in the future.

You need at least 40 trades on an excellent performance report. As you can see from the table above, 200 businesses are optimal since the margin of error decreases fast from 14% to 7% with only an additional 150 trades.

If you test your system on more than 200 trades, the margin of error decreases at a slower rate. The next 100 transactions only increase the confidence by 2%.

Principle #10: Choose a Valid Back-Testing Period

I recently saw the following ad:

> "*Since 1994, I've taught thousands of traders worldwide a simple and reliable E-mini trading methodology.*"

That's an exciting claim…

The E-mini S&P was introduced in September of 1997. The E-mini NASDAQ was introduced in June of 1999; therefore, NONE of these contracts existed before 1997.

Regardless, though, we only have to worry about the age of the contracts for back-testing purposes. If you develop an E-mini S&P trading strategy, you should only back-test it for the past 3-4 years anyway.

It is because, even though the contract has existed since 1997, there was practically nobody trading it (see the following chart):

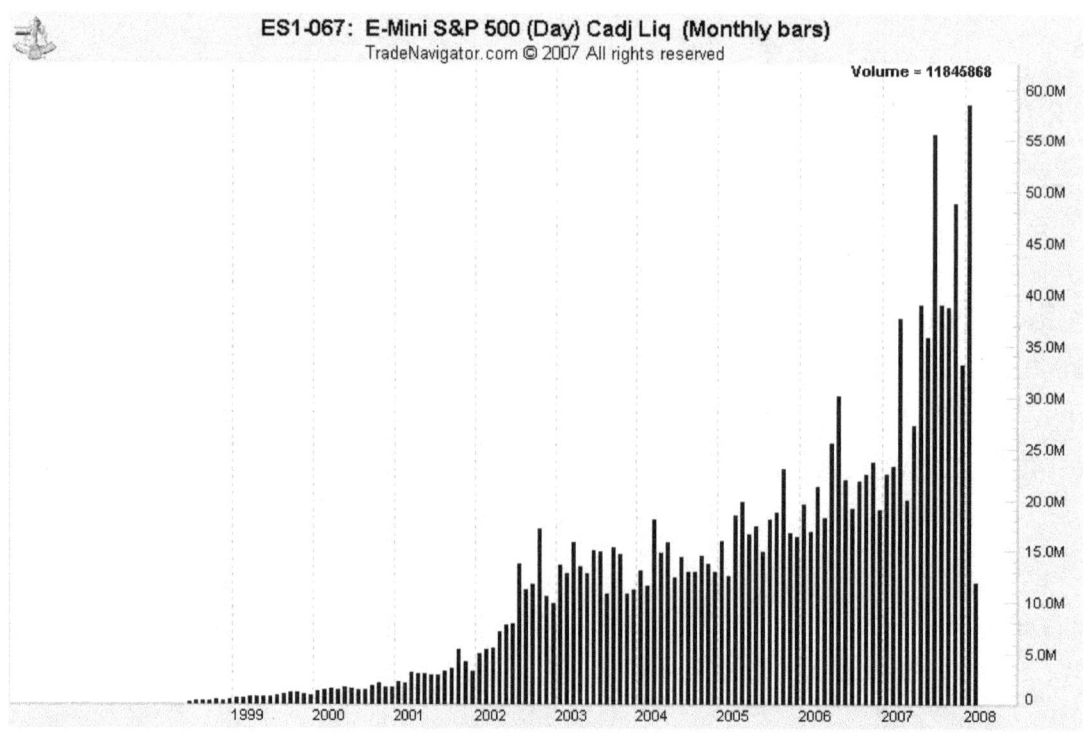

The same applies to strategies for the grain futures: they were introduced in August of 2006. Do not make the mistake of back-testing your trading strategy on the pit contract. When futures contracts start trading electronically, they attract a different kind of trader than their pit-traded counterparts; therefore, the two markets' characteristics can be very other.

It would not be brilliant to think that the markets remain the same once they can be electronically traded. Faster fills and lower commissions allow a different kind of trading strategy. The markets WILL behave differently than when only pit traders sold them.

Action Items:

Take a look at your trading strategy and run it against these 10 Power Principles. How many principles apply?

If your trading strategy doesn't fulfill all 10 Principles, is there any area to improve it?

****

Chapter 12

There's More To Trading Than Just Having a Strategy

Congratulations. You made it to the third part of the book. You've learned about the basics of day trading, and you know how to develop a profitable trading strategy.

You understand that a profitable trading strategy is one of the single most important factors for your trading.

With a proven, reliable strategy, you'll have a map for your trading future and a guideline for your success. You'll have a plan. Most traders out there open a trading account and start trading without knowing what they're getting themselves into. Only a few of them have a trading strategy, and because of that, many of them fail.

The vast majority of them fail. According to a report from the North American Securities Administrators Association (NASAA):

> *"Only 11.5% [of traders] might profitably trade [the markets]. At least 70% of traders lose money in the markets...70% of public traders will not only lose but will almost certainly lose everything they invest."*

At least 70% will lose everything they invest. And only 11.5% of traders will succeed. That's just slightly over 1 in 10. Not great odds.

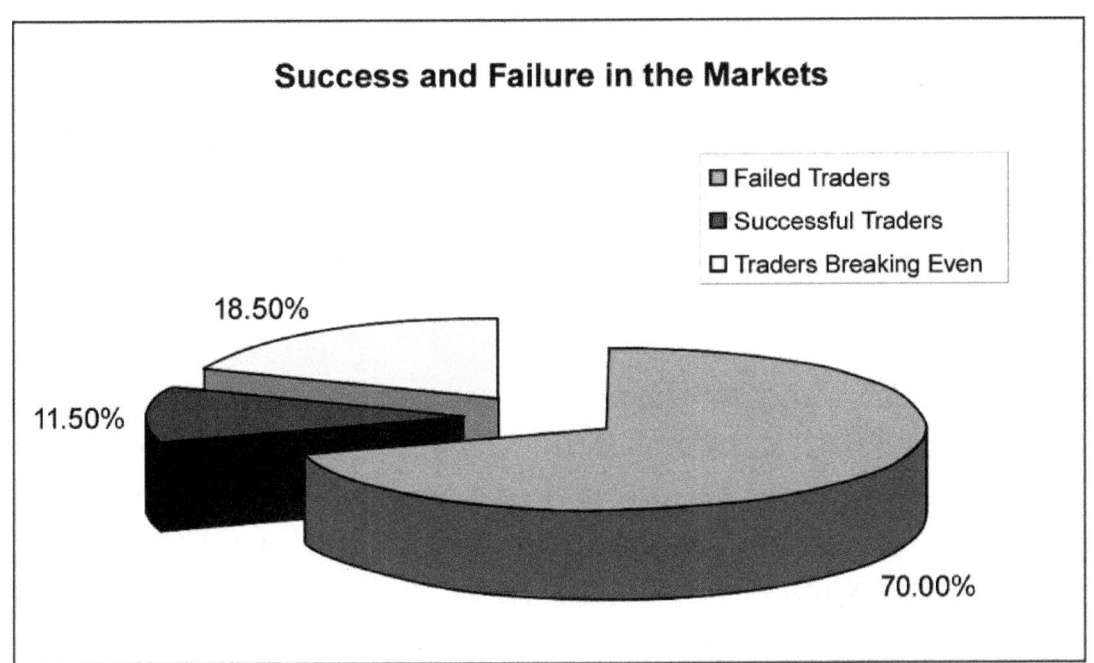

But, if you've followed the action items outlined throughout the previous chapters, then you should have a trading strategy mapped out. And, if you do, then that small step has dramatically increased your chances of belonging to the 11.5% of successful traders out there who are making money.

But here's the thing about trading strategies: they're a dime a dozen.

These days, you can find hundreds of books with different trading strategies, along with countless websites that offer trading strategies for free. You'll also find "the trading strategy of the month" every couple of weeks in nearly every trading industry magazine out there.

So, if there are so many trading strategies available, why do only 11.5% of traders make money?

The problem is that strategies do NOT make a profitable trader. There's more to trading than just having a plan. Only time, knowledge, experience, and guidance can earn you the trader you want to be.

The Ralph Vince Experiment

Ralph Vince is a well-respected and well-known financial investor and educator. He's published several books on trading and the trading industry. He also performed a very famous experiment known as the Ralph Vince Experiment.

Mr. Vince took 40 Ph. D.s and set them up to trade with a computer game. Now, these 40 people all had doctorates. Still, Mr. Vince made sure that none of their doctorates involved any background in statistics or trading. Each of them was given $1,000 and 100 trades in the game, with a 60% winning percentage. When they won, they won the amount of money they risked. When they lost, they lost the amount of money they bet. Simple. As you can see, ALL of them had a profitable trading strategy.

So, after all, 40 had completed their 100 trades, how many do you think made money?
2. Only two doctorates out of 40 were able to make money. The other 38 failed to succeed.

Source: CSI News Journal, March 1992

Those are pretty convincing statistics. 95% of the candidates lost out. And why? Because they fell into the age-old traps: poor money management, gambler's fallacy, and lack of discipline, guidance, and experience.

Did they have a profitable trading strategy? Of course!

Remember, each one of the traders took 100 trades with a 60% winning percentage. Mr. Vince gave them a profitable trading strategy to use, but they still couldn't succeed.
So, it seems that there is more to trading than just having a strategy. And that's what you'll learn about in this section of the book:
The OTHER factors that are involved when it comes to your trading success.

Chapter 13

The Seven Mistakes of Traders and How to Avoid Them

So, let's examine why traders fail. If you know the pitfalls of trading, then it becomes easier to avoid them. In this chapter, we'll talk about the mistakes traders make and how you can prevent them.

First off, there are two types of mistakes that a trader can make:

- The small ones
- The big ones

Yes, you'll make small mistakes along the way – I guarantee it. You might buy a security when you intended to sell it, simply because you pushed the wrong button. Or maybe you'll buy the wrong stock just because there's a typo when you enter the symbol. Another possibility is placing the wrong order because you enter a buy order at $213.5 instead of $21.35. These types of things have happened to all of us.

They're small mistakes, and they're "forgivable." With a little bit of luck, you might even be able to profit from them.

However, there are big mistakes that you absolutely MUST avoid if you're going to be a successful trader.

For instance, one of the biggest trading mistakes you could ever make is trying to learn and understand everything about trading…and then never actually START to trade.

I know many aspiring traders who have read countless books, have developed dozens of trading strategies, and have analyzed several markets. Still, they've failed to pull the trigger when it comes to real trading. As you know, part of your education is your knowledge and your experience. If you want to make money with trading, you eventually have to take the plunge and get started.

Yes, I know: there's a chance of losing some money. That's true. When you trade, you're taking a risk. (If you want to know how to start selling without risking any of your own money, please read the chapter "How to Start Trading Without Risking a Single Penny,"

What Exactly Is "Risk?"

Risk means "not having control." Example: If you're driving a car on the highway, then you're at risk. It's as simple as that. But, thankfully, there are certain things we can do to control that risk:

All motorists are required to have a formal education and successfully test their driving skills before they are allowed to drive a car. This qualification process is called getting a driver's license.

Cars are equipped with certain security features, such as seat belts, airbags, anti-brake systems, and – let's not forget – a steering wheel, which enables you to navigate around obstacles in your path.

When you're new to driving, you usually practice with another person (e.g. your parent) in an empty parking lot BEFORE hitting the road. You start driving at 10 mph, and then, as you grow more comfortable, you can slowly increase the speed. When you're confident in your abilities, you'll most likely leave the parking lot for the open road (but let's not move too fast – probably a country road, with no traffic!)

All of these things help you control the risk when it comes to driving. You'll never be able to eliminate the risk completely, but you can take appropriate action to reduce it. The same principles apply in trading:

You should have a formal education and prove your skills before you start to trade. Unfortunately, there are no tests required before you can open a brokerage account, but you should take the time to learn about the markets and develop a strategy before you "hit the open road." When trading, you can also apply certain "security features." Two of the most important are having a trading strategy and using stop losses.

When you're new to trading, you should paper trade first.

Then, after you've built up some confidence, you can start trading with one lot/contract, or 100 shares. If you're comfortable and you achieve acceptable results, then you can increase the contract or share size. And never trade with money you can't afford to lose. Get your current financial situation in order first, and THEN start trading.

Get your credit cleaned up, pay off high interest loans and credit cards, and put at least three months of living expenses in savings. Once this is done, you're ready to start letting your money work for you.

Don't trade to get rich quick. That's the number one principle when it comes to controlling your risk.

If day trading were easy, everyone in the world would be doing the same thing: trading like crazy every day and becoming insanely rich by nightfall!

We both know it's NOT easy. So let's take a look at the seven "deadly" trading mistakes. These are the challenges that every trader faces, and they're the ones that usually cost traders a lot of money.

Being aware of these challenges is the first step in avoiding them. Think about the car driving example again: if you know that driving on icy roads is dangerous, you can avoid traveling in that particular weather condition. But, if you don't know about ice and the hazard it poses, you might just get into your car and drive like normal. You won't even realize the danger until you feel your vehicle slipping right off the road.

The same principle applies in trading: being aware of the possible mistakes and pitfalls will help you avoid them.

Mistake #1: Struggling To Identify the Direction of the Market

Traders use very complicated formulas, indicators, and systems to identify a trend. They'll plot so many hands on the screen that they can't even see the prices anymore.

They think that the more complicated a system is, the better it should "predict" the trends.

As a result, they completely lose sight of the basic principle: buy when the market is going up and sell when the market goes down.

About Indicators

These days, there are more than 150 indicators available, and you can even get hands for indicators. Keep in mind that indicators are based on five variables: the open, the high, the low, the close, and the volume of a specific timeframe.

Indicators are merely collecting this data and displaying it differently. They do this by setting certain variables up concerning others or concerning previous data.

Examples:
- Williams %R displays the high and the low to the close.
- Moving Averages show the relationship between a series of closing prices over some time.

Remember, keep it simple:

One of the easiest ways to identify a trend is to use trendlines. In the section "Technical Indicators," you've been shown exactly how to construct and use trendlines.

Mistake #2: Not Taking Profits

By their very nature, traders are greedy. After all, you want to make money. A lot of money. And you want to make it fast. "Get rich quick," right? Every trader wants to get rich, and they want to do it in one trade.
And that's when they lose.

Trading success comes from consistency, not from a trading "grand slam."

There are a lot of newbie traders out there who believe that their fortune will be made in just one fantastic trade, and then they'll never have to work again for their entire life.

It is a dream, a dangerous one. Successful traders will realize that right away.

The best, and usually only, way to make a fortune in trading is consistency. And this fortune will probably be made in small amounts. Unfortunately, most traders go for the big wins, which result in significant losses.

It makes sense that traders are more interested in more enormous profits per trade. What would you rather have – a fifty dollar bill or a five-dollar bill? Well, that's obvious! But when it comes to trading, it's not that simple. If you DON'T take the five-dollar account, you may lose fifty dollars of your OWN money or more.

The main thing to keep in mind is this: even though you can't take the fifty dollar bill right away, you can take ten five-dollar bills over a longer time. And the result is the same – fifty dollars.

And that's the main point here: small, steady profits add up. It is not to say you'll never have a big winner. For example, in options trading, it's pretty common to have 100%, 200%, or even 1,000% in just one trade. So, it's not impossible to snag the big profits – it's just not something you should count on. If you expect numbers like this all the time and accept nothing less, you're setting yourself up for guaranteed disappointment.

The key to trading success: small but consistent profits. Consistency is the key. If your earnings are consistent and predictable, you can use leverage to trade size.

Therefore, you MUST know when to exit with a profit. Resist the temptation to stay in "just a little longer, for just a little more."

Mistake #3: Not Limiting Your Losses

The only way you can make a fortune with trading is actually to stay in the game, and it's hard to stay in the game when you've already lost all of your dough.

Losses are a part of our business. The key to trading success is to limit your losses. Too many traders are giving a trade way too much "room," and they're taking big hits, which can shrink an account down by 20%, 30%, and sometimes even 40%. Set small losses.

As outlined in the chapter "Is It Possible to Make a Living As a Day Trader?", your average loss should be smaller than your average win because then you'll be making profits even if your winning percentage is only 50%.

Always know when to exit a trade.

Mistake #4: Trading the Wrong Market

Too many traders are fixed on only one market; they trade ONLY the forex USD/EUR, or the E-mini Russell, or the E-mini DOW, or just individual stocks, etc.

Here's another key to trading success: trade a MOVING market, either up or down. You know you should buy when the market goes up and sell when the market goes down.

So stay away from a choppy market or just moving sideways, and start trading a market with social trends.

Take a look at the following examples:

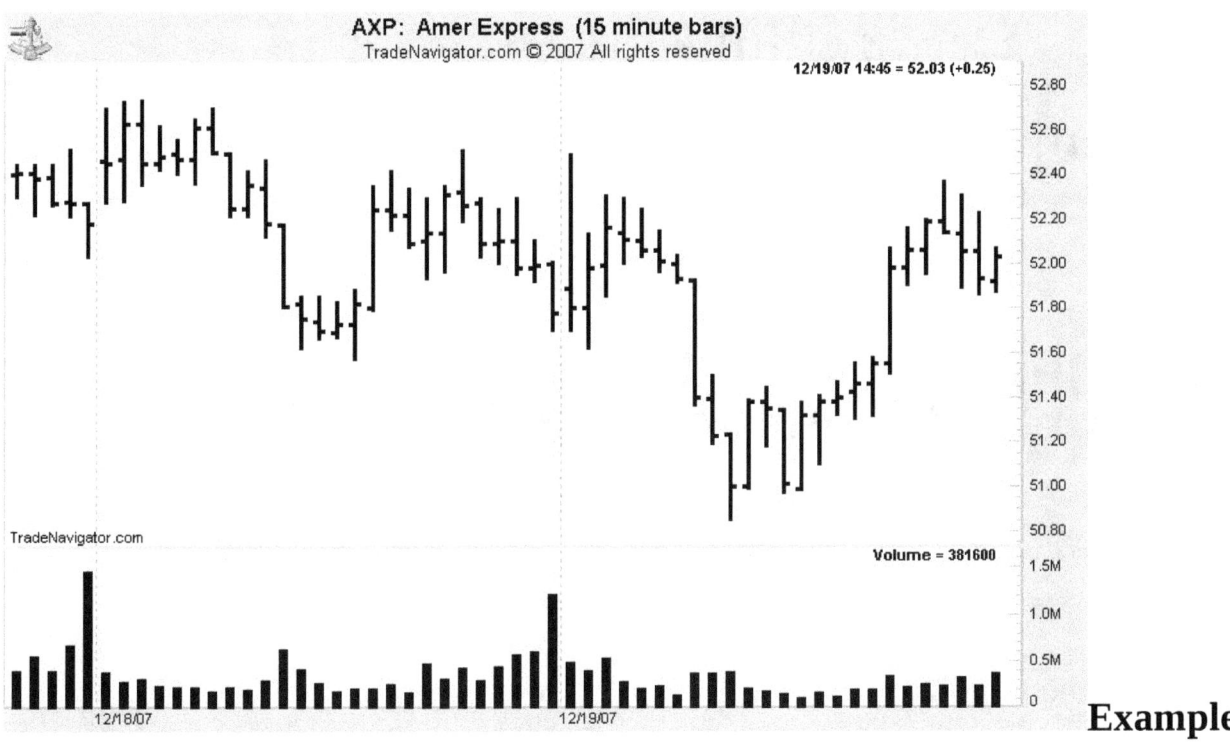

Example 1: Choppy Market

Choppy Market

Example 2: Trending Market:

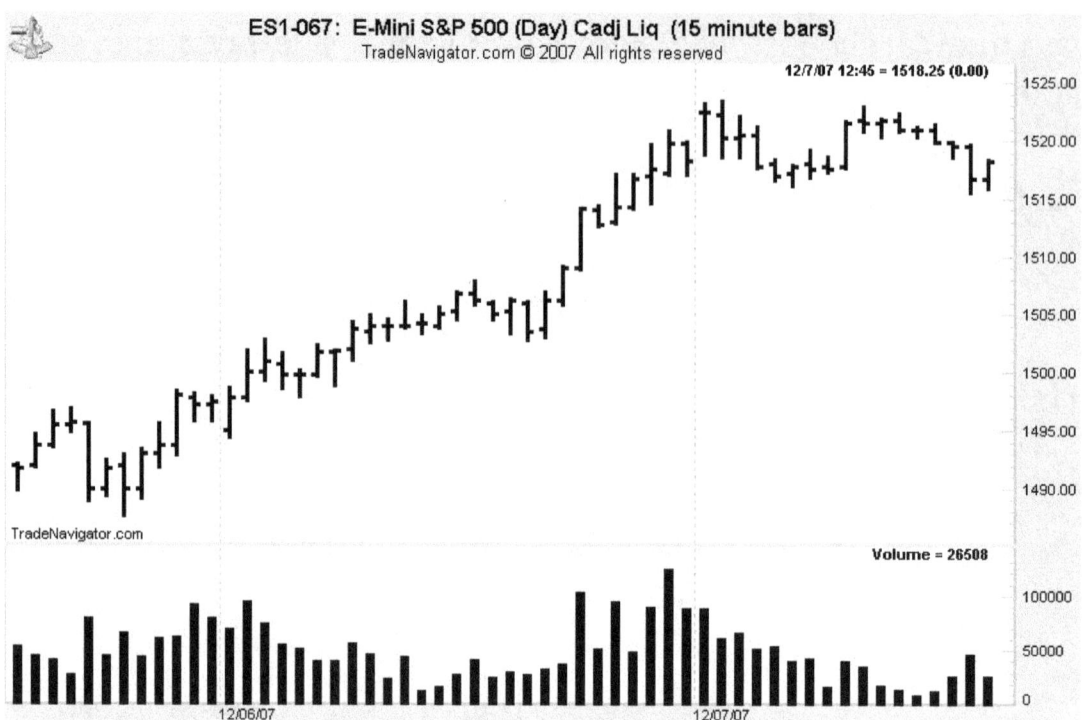

Trending Market

Stick with the trending market, and you'll find the profits you're after.

Mistake #5: Lack of a Trading Strategy

You MUST have a solid trading strategy. Having a trading strategy is probably the most critical thing you can do to succeed with trading. Having a trading strategy means having a pre-defined set of rules that you have developed for your day trading.

It means knowing what you're doing instead of just gambling. Too many people start day trading without a strategy, which means that they're completely unprepared.

With a day trading strategy, you're way ahead of the crowd, and you've dramatically increased your chances of making money with trading.

Mistake #6: Not Controlling Your Emotions

What are the primary emotions of traders? There are many! Here's just a few:

- Greed – "I'm sure the market will continue rising, and I'll make millions!"

- Fear – "Please…. I don't want to experience another loss."

- Panic – "Oh no, the market is moving fast. Why? What should I do? The sky is falling…!"

- Indecision – "Should I enter this trade? Or should I wait? Ok, now I'm in a trade: should I take profits? Or not yet? Hmm, the trade goes against me: should I get out now, or should I give it a little bit more room?"

- Excitement (hopefully!) – "Hey, I made money!"

How many negative emotions are on this list? Too many!

To become a successful trader, you have to have control over your emotions. The best strategies and tools are useless if you lose your head while you're in a trade.

The Best Tools Are Useless

I recently saw the movie "The Guardian" with Kevin Costner and Ashton Kutcher. It's about the U.S. Coast Guard. Kevin Costner plays an instructor who trains young recruits to become rescue swimmers.

One day, they have a simple exercise in the pool: one of the instructors simulates a victim, and one of the cadets has to rescue him. When the rescue swimmer approaches the drowning victim, the victim grabs the swimmer and holds him tight, trying not to drown.

The rescue swimmer panics and can't escape the victim's grip. And both of them almost drown.

After the exercise, Kevin Costner's character explains this to the cadets; the only difference between THEM and the drowning victim out there in the ocean is that THEY have a strategy to rescue the victim and deal with the situation. But all of the tools and equipment they have are useless if they panic or have no idea what to do.

They need to remain calm and execute their strategy.

The same is true in trading: you can have the best trading strategy, superior software, the fastest computer, several 21" monitors, a $1,500 ergonomic chair, and an office with the most stunning view, but all of these things are useless if you're in a trade and you panic.

Remain calm, cool, and relaxed. Control your emotions – don't let them control you.

Mistake #7: Overtrading

Many traders think that "quantity" is better than "quality." They believe that if you just throw enough punches, one will eventually hit. They trade like maniacs and make their broker rich.

Traders are overtrading for the following three reasons, and none of them are good:

1.) **Greed**

> You just closed a winning trade. You followed your plan and made the profits that you were looking for. But the market keeps going up. You think, "I should have stayed in this trade," so you jump right

back in. And then you realize that YOU were the one who just bought the high of the day.

2.) Revenge

You lost money. The market has been mean to you. "They" just took out your stop, and now the market keeps moving in your direction. So you want to get back at them. You keep trading, thinking, "The next trade will make back all the money I lost so far, and that will hurt them." Believe me: the market is ALWAYS more substantial, and it will be YOU who gets the bloody nose.

3.) Boredom

There are some days when the ducks simply don't line up. You're watching the markets, and it's like watching paint dry: nothing moves. You wait…and wait…and wait…and suddenly you get that "itch" to trade. You think, "If I don't trade, I won't make any money!" and you jump into a trade immediately. Of course, the transaction isn't according to your plan, and you end up with a loss.

I have some news for you: if you don't trade when there's nothing to sell, then you won't lose any money – guaranteed!

If you want to succeed in trading, then you must understand the concept of taking only the "high-probability trades." Less is more.

Follow your plan!

****

Chapter 14

The Trader's Psyche

You know that you need a strategy. And you know that there's more to trading than just having a system. In the previous chapter, you learned about the significant mistakes that traders make. You learned that your biggest enemy is not another trader, or market makers, or your broker – it's YOU.

And YOU are your biggest enemy because of your **emotions.**

In this chapter, you'll learn about the mindset and psyche of successful traders. Having a profitable trading strategy AND the right attitude will catapult you right into the 11.5% successful traders we talked about earlier.

To develop the right mindset, you need to know what to expect when day trading.

Many traders mistakenly believe that trading will result in a consistently rising account balance, like having an ATM in their front yard.

But you already know that losses are a part of our business as traders. There will be some days and weeks when your trading exceeds your expectations, and there will be periods when your trading results are far worse than you expected.

You must maintain a long-term perspective.

Day trading means playing a numbers game. You already know that you need to place at least 40 trades before you can look at the strategy's performance. Most traders only evaluate their account once a month, trying to have as many profitable months as possible. Hedge funds evaluate their performances quarterly or yearly.

Long-term evaluations have their place, but it will drive you crazy if you look at your trading results daily. That's why we define weekly goals.

Sure, nobody likes going through a drawdown. But when you're trading, it's inevitable. The key is in how you deal with it.

In an interview with Jack D. Schwager for his book, <u>Market Wizards: Interviews With Top Traders</u>, the famous Richard Dennis said:

> *"It is counterproductive to get wrapped up in the results. You have to maintain your perspective. Being emotionally deflated would mean lacking confidence in what I am doing. I avoid that because I have always felt that it is misleading to focus on short-term results."*

And way too many traders focus on short-term results and lose their perspective. That's why they fail: they experience a loss or a bad week, and so they start trading a different strategy. And while the trading strategy they just abandoned is recovering from the drawdown, the new trading strategy may result in yet more losses, so again, they start looking for another.

It's like a dog chasing too many rabbits: at the end of the day, he's exhausted, and he has absolutely nothing to show for it because he missed a single thing.

Day trading necessitates selective, wise, and patient trading methods. Successful day traders are practical and do not go overboard when trading the market. They focus on the quality of each trade, not the quantity.

Here are some essential characteristics of successful traders:

1.) **Successful traders do not blame.** They accept their losses, and they don't dwell on them or blame other people or conditions. They learn from their mistakes and move on with their trading.

2.) **Successful traders have a system.** They stick to their method of trading religiously.

3.) **Successful traders have patience.** They know that most positions will not be profitable the minute they are opened.

4.) **Successful traders do not overtrade.** They realize that overtrading puts their account at risk, and they know that not every day is a day for trading. They wait for high probability opportunities.

5.) **Successful traders realize that nothing is 100% foolproof.** They trust in their indicators, but they are aware of other factors that may influence their trades.

6.) **Successful traders do not stay in a losing trade.** They honor the stop losses that they set, and they do not hold their position in the hopes that the market will eventually "go their way."

7.) **Successful traders do not rush into trades.** They take their time while selecting businesses, and they are picky about which trades to jump on. They don't place orders just for the sake of having a position in the market every second.

8.) **Successful traders stick to a successful strategy.** They have one to three techniques that work, and they use them repeatedly and repeatedly.

9.) **Successful traders can adapt.** They adjust their trading methods and decisions to changing market conditions.

10.) **Successful traders know what type of trader they are.** They don't force themselves to trade with methods or strategies that do not fit their personality.

11.) **Successful traders bank on consistent profits.** They know that ignoring the small-profit trades and angling for a "grand slam" is a sure way to lose money.

12.) **Successful traders take action.** They don't let their fear control their decisions or interfere with their trading.

13.) **Successful traders use successful systems.** Their trading methods and indicators focus on high probability trades, sound money management, keeping their strategies free of curve-fitting, and working their design into their business plans for successful implementation.

14.) **Successful traders recognize a "good" trade.** They don't base their evaluation on profits or losses; they base it on whether or not they followed their trading plan to the letter. Even if they lose money, as long as they stuck to their goal, it is a "good" trade.

15.) **Successful traders take time off.** They realize the importance of taking breaks from trading and the markets to clear their heads.

16.) **Successful traders do not fear losses.** They realize that failures are a part of their business, and they expect them.

If you can adopt the right psychological mindset, you'll gain a significant edge in the market.

I can't stress this enough:

The right mindset is one of the keys to investment success, and most traders fail to understand this.

Greed and Fear

When day trading, two emotions are always present: greed and fear. If your trade goes well, your natural inclination will be to trade even more, opening yourself up to a significant loss. And if your business goes wrong, fear will torture you. Fear of failure or fear of a further loss makes traders scared.

Greed and fear are destructive emotions. They influence all traders; they're a natural part of every trader's psychology. Desire and anxiety can make traders act irrationally: they may know what they should do, but they can't do it.

The bottom line: if you're scared or greedy, and you can't control your emotions when day trading, then you'll have a challenging time being profitable.

But, you will have a fantastic chance of success with your trading plan when you trade well. Feel proud of yourself for profitable trades and decisions, but don't dwell on them or allow arrogance to set in. Keep your head up and continue to apply a sound trading strategy, even when you suffer losses – remember, they are just a part of the business.

Do not allow yourself to get caught up in positive or negative emotions – understand the psychology behind trading and know that no trade is guaranteed.

Work on your mental state. If a trade goes wrong, try and work out why it did, and learn from it. Executing a trading method with discipline is the only way to overcome destructive emotions. Whether you're a day trader or an investor, and whether you trade in commodities, stocks, or currencies, the fact is that your trading psychology WILL influence your results.

It would be best if you never traded without a solid reason. Don't chase the market. If a market moves sharply, but you don't participate in this move because your entry criteria weren't met, don't worry about it. If you miss a trade, another one will be just around the corner. Practice patience and discipline.

It would be best if you control your emotions by having a specific plan to follow. Having the correct trading psychology is just as important as having a reliable trading strategy.

The more you are prepared mentally for trading, the better you will trade. Note my emphasis on better trading, not better winning. Profits do not define a good day in day trading. Successful day traders define a good day as researched and planned and follow their overall trading strategy.

Action Items:

The "Law of Attraction" says that "you get what you think about." Here's how to avoid negative emotions and to have a positive attitude:

Write down 10 "I Am" statements. These statements should reflect who you WANT to be, not necessarily who you are now.

Here are some examples of "I Am" statements:

- I am a disciplined trader who follows his trading plan.
- I am calm and relaxed when I am trading.
- I am in control of my emotions.
- I am a profitable trader.

Read these "I Am" statements every morning before you start trading. Read them aloud and read them as you mean it. Do it for two weeks, and I promise, you WILL notice a difference.

****

Chapter 15

The Three "Secrets" to Day Trading Success

Trading can be simple, but it's not easy. And trading is more difficult if you complicate it. Remember the saying: "A Confused Mind Takes No Action." As a trader, you MUST take action every day; therefore, you must avoid confusion.

So could you keep it simple? Very simple.

Here are the three "Secrets" to Day Trading Success

1.) **Secret 1: Trading In the Right Direction**

   You must buy when the market is going up and sell when the market is going down. That's how money is made.

2.) **Secret 2: Always Know When To Exit A Trade**

   It is essential that you know when it's the right time to exit with a profit AND when it's the right time to leave with a loss.

3.) **Secret 3: Trade the Right Market**

   The right market is a trending market. As you know, money is made in trends – either up or down – so you dramatically increase your chances of making money if you trade a trending market.

Now you know why I put the word "secrets" in quotation marks. These are not "secrets" at all. Unfortunately, most traders don't realize the importance of these facts and tend to forget them.

Losing traders focus on finding a "magic method" of trading, visiting countless websites, and spending hundreds and thousands of dollars on books, courses, and software packages.

Don't make the same mistake. Keep your trading simple.

Remember, the "secrets" to day trading success are universal. They apply to every market, whether you're trading stocks, futures, options, or forex.
And they apply to every timeframe, which is why they're so powerful.

Focus on the "secrets:"

1.) Learn how to determine whether the market is going up or going down.

2.) Learn when to exit a trade, when to make a profit, and when to bail if the market is not moving in your favor.

3.) And learn how to find the right market.

Don't make your trading overly complicated. Stick to the basics. As you already know, if you can't drive a Ford, you won't be able to drive a Ferrari. And if you can't drive a car at ten mph, you shouldn't try to go it at 80mph.

Remember Power Principle #1: Use Few Rules – Make It Easy to Understand (page 192). That's how your trading plan should be.

Action Items:
Take a look at your trading plan right now and answer the following questions:

Have you found an easy way to identify the direction of the market?

What tools or indicators are you using?

Are you using more than two indicators? Are they complimenting each other or contradicting each other?

Can you describe your entry rules in two lines or less?

- Do you know exactly when to exit a trade?

- Do you know when to exit a trade even before you enter it?

- Are you sure you're trading the right market? Did you select a call based on your goals or based on a "friend's" recommendation?

Did you evaluate other markets to see if there's an alternative market that may support your goals? Moreover your trading strategy BETTER than the one you're trading now?

****